D1328231

CLIMBING THE SUMMIT

The true story of a Black boy's dreams in a rich White town

Anthony Ellis

First edition 2022

ISBN 979-8-9859805-1-6 (paperback)

DEDICATION

To my family, Johane, Adrien, and Celine,

My mother, Evelyn, Norman, and my brothers Tyrone and Cory,

Thank you for all your love and support.

To my friends and the town of Summit,

You've become a part of me.

CONTENTS

Author's Note

To write this book, I relied upon my own memories, perspective, journals, stories, and researched facts when I could. The events and conversations in this book have been set down to the best of my ability.

I consulted with several of the people who appear in the book. The names of some of the individuals were changed in this book, and in some cases identifying details were modified in order to protect the privacy of individuals. There are no composite characters. I occasionally omitted people and events, and compressed time, but only when it had no impact on the substance of the story.

I can be contacted at the following:
Instagram: instragram.com/anthonyellisauthor
Facebook: facebook.com/anthonyellisauthor

Instructions

E-book:

FOR ADDITIONAL EXPERIENCE: The electronic book version includes interactions accessible through technology and internet service including linkages to media throughout the book. Clink the highlighted linked words and images to activate the associated media (e.g., Instagram, YouTube). Return to the story by returning to this book manually. There is no automated linkage to bring you back to the story.

Hardcover & Paperback:

FOR ADDITIONAL EXPERIENCE: The physical version of this book will not allow automated interactions through technology in its paper form. To access the media and related linkages, please refer and scan the QR Codes at bottom of pages where media is referred. The QR Codes are tied to the numbers in the text and will direct the reader to playlists of media mentioned and a specific media, in some cases. The reader will then be required to access the media through a separate means of technology.

A Dream Deferred

What happens to a dream deferred?

Does it dry up

Like a raisin in the sun?

Or fester like a sore--

And then run?

Does it stink like rotten meat?

Or crust and sugar over--

like a syrupy sweet?

Maybe it just sags

like a heavy load.

Or does it explode?

    -   Langston Hughes

Introduction

Run! The thought pushed frigid fall air out of my mouth like a last breath of life. The black and blue uniforms of the cops came closer into view between the suburban homes to the field of gravel, mud, and grass where we were.

"Stop! Freeze!" the police yelled. My White friends disappeared quickly as I scanned for a path to take: the train tracks in the distance were dangerous with trains on them, and I didn't know where the woods to my right would lead me. I chose the sky-high fence as a feat I could conquer to get away. I was made for this. I grabbed my sagging pants and launched into a sprint. My teenage legs were the fastest; they had to help me. I couldn't get caught. I was supposed to be the Black boy that goes to college . . .

Molded Cheese

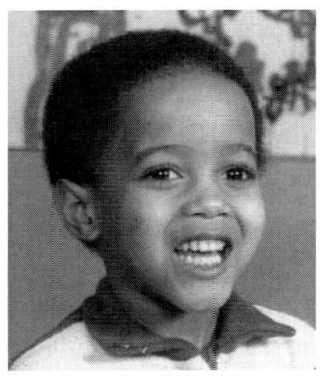

Molded cheese.

That's what came to mind as I sat in my English class at Jefferson elementary school in the 1980s. I recalled my young eleven years of life up until that point.

As a child, I lived at my grandparents' house with my mom and two older brothers, Tyrone and Cory, in the affluent suburbs of Summit, New Jersey. My mom named me Anthony so I would have a less ethnic name than my brothers.

Our house was a two-family home near other modest Black families in a neighborhood at the bottom of Summit's hill. The town seemed better as you ascended past pristine parks and some of the best schools in the state. On the main road were fancy clothing shops, sweet bakeries, pizzerias, and money-filled banks. Views of New York City were in the distance. Streets led up to mansions at the top of town where White people lived, near the clouds and sun.

Still, the sun came through trees into the windows of our home. Tyrone and I woke up on bunk beds and my oldest brother Cory was on a bed within arm's reach, all of us in one room. Since I was two years younger than Ty, I had the top bed. I nearly hit my head on the ceiling when Mom flung open the door. She had already straightened up her bed on the couch in the living room, pressed her hair into a pouf, put on her glasses, and got dressed in Aunt Esther's room which was next to ours.

"Tony, Tyrone, and Cory, time to get up," Mom said.

Cory was nearly ten years older than me and towered over Mom when he stood up to get dressed. Ty and I wiped the crust from our eyes while the sun came through the window. We got clothes out the dresser in the hallway near the door to the attic and door to the neighbor's side of the duplex house. Aunt Esther and Grandpa were still using the only bathroom, so we had to wait for them to finish.

The smell of pancakes and bacon filled the house because Grandma was up making Grandpa breakfast downstairs. I ran down and sat at the table dancing while munching on Cap'n Crunch.

My uncle Clift came out from sleeping on his couch in the basement next to the pool table. He smacked me upside the head, "Boy, stop dancing and eat your food."

I knew he loved me as I glanced at the newspaper clipping on the fridge of me holding an award from the picture, he helped me draw.

After stuffing down breakfast, I scurried out the back door as fast as I could. My brothers said hi to my cousins Hakim and his older brother Aman as they came over from their home, my Aunt Jeanette's apartment, next door. My cousin Steven arrived with his mom, Aunt Yvonne, from his apartment a few blocks away. We all grinned and knew it was time to do what we always do: play basketball.

"A game of 21?" Tyrone asked.

We all nodded and agreed. Tyrone started the game dribbling from the foul line, taking it in for a layup. Cory grabbed the rebound using his giant body, which was fit to play football. Mom wouldn't let him play so he could keep his focus on school. Tyrone had the muscles and skill to score a few times. Hakim and Steve were my age. Hakim did his signature move of dribbling behind his back then missed the shot. Steve grabbed the rebound then hugged the ball while he was slapped and fouled. We sweat and breathed heavily with excitement as Aman used his strength to lay up and scored. Uncle Clift came out the house running onto the court, and we all smiled to see him play with us as he jumped high, snatched a rebound, spun around and scored, then left.

I was a skinny pencil quickly dribbling through my legs as my heart thumped, reminding me what my doctor said a couple years ago: "He has a heart murmur; I can't approve him to play sports for school." I played on, for now.

Tyrone yelled, "I got nineteen!"

Everyone looked at him in disbelief then defended him until he scored and won.

We ran all over the yard. Grandpa was fixing his 1960s Thunderbird car. We hoped he'd teach us to play pool again in the basement later. The next-door neighbor's dog barked at us from inside, instilling fear that he'd come outside to chase us. A shed near the garden still had burn marks on it from when my cousin Hassan and Tyrone nearly burned it down. On the ground were our BMX bikes we used to jump ramps and ride down to Bryant Pond. By the side of the house was a grill and tables for when we had barbecues with juicy ribs, hamburgers, and hot dogs. Next door was the church Grandma went to every Sunday wearing her custom-made hats with lace and feathers. On the front lawn, we played football where Cory launched the ball to us and we tackled each other aggressively, sometimes getting angry.

Grandma watched us proudly from the porch with our mothers; they raised us together like we were all their children. My mom and her siblings grew up together, eight of them. They were brought from a good education in segregated schools in Virginia to a smaller home up north for a better life and education in Summit. Grandma told my mom growing up, "We're just as good as White people; we just gotta work harder."

Now, she shouted at us at her home in a predominately White town, "Y'all don't fight each other; y'all family!" We nodded with respect.

We sat down near the sidewalk to watch expensive, shiny cars drive by and yelled out which one we wanted, filling our heads with dreams of riches. I gazed at planes flying above cutting through the clouds

imitated Chaka Khan when singing "I Feel For You," as I tried to breakdance to the song. Then we relaxed for a moment when Mom put on her favorite song "Giving You The Best that I've Got" by Anita Baker while she and Grandma sat at the dining room table.

The spotlight always seemed to be on me as I'd spent years trying to make my family smile. I stood in front of them when Michael Jackson's[3] song "Billie Jean" played on the radio. I lip synched, "Billie Jean is not my lover," as I kicked my feet like I had on Michael's shiny black loafers, white socks, and a glittery white glove on my hand while twisting my hips as they smiled and clapped. Their eyes glimmered and focused on me; I felt special, and nothing else mattered in the world but that moment.

Aunt Esther had a baby named Devin who was living with us at Grandma's. He was there, growing over the years. He was in the background, crawling then walking in the living room while I tried to dance for the

 3

family. Their eyes moved to him. He walked towards them with his watermelon head, curly hair, and pudgy cheeks. They gave him hugs and kisses while my dancing was pushed into a dark corner away from their sight. I thought, *Geez, everyone loves him. What about me?* I became enraged. No one was paying me any attention. I was no longer important.

One day, Grandpa dropped me off at Jefferson Elementary School, and I went to my English class. My teacher told us to write about anything we wanted. I gazed up at her as she stood in front of the class with long blonde hair and bell bottom pants. I pressed my pencil into the paper on the desk as my feet dangled. The other kids had their heads down with their pencils scribbling away on paper as I looked out the window at the sun and trees outside. I didn't know what they were thinking. Like me, their dreams of flying away into the skies like Superman were starting to fade away as we got older.

I frowned when remembering how my family treated me with Devin around now.

I was ignored, forgotten, and projected an image to write about how I felt: a yellow block of cheddar in the back of my grandmother's fridge with spots of green furry fungus.

I squeezed the pencil and feverishly put down my feelings and words, as they appeared on the paper like magic.

I wrote something like this:

I love my family,

But when my little cousin was born

I felt like molded cheese.

As the writing finished, the jealousy of my cousin faded, and a sense of satisfaction warmed me. I glowed at the paper in front of me. I gave it to my teacher, and she gave me a check plus for the assignment. I happily put it in my bag and went to Grandma's house.

When I got home, I sat my backpack on the chair in the living room, slightly open like usual, and went back outside to play . . .

"Tony!" my mom yelled for me.

I came running inside. "Yeah?" I said.

My Mom, Aunt Esther, Grandma, and Uncle Clift were all sitting around the dining room table smiling, gleaming like I'd done something miraculous.

"So, you felt like molded cheese, huh?" my mom said, smirking.

"Uhh, what? Why did you read that? I didn't want you to read it."

I walked away to the couch in the living room with my mouth poked out and my face heated in embarrassment.

My mom came in and sat next to me. "What's wrong? I didn't know you felt this way."

"You made fun of me," I said.

"I'm sorry. It's good though; I'm proud of you for expressing yourself. Keep it up." Her words lingered around me like a gentle breeze. I gripped hold of the feeling as it embraced my body. I felt better.

I made my mother proud. My absent father couldn't be proud though since he chose not to be with us.

My family's eyes sparkled in that moment. Their gaze was on me.

I'd done something that no one else could do. I was different. And I sat and wondered about the magic I created in those few words. They felt how I felt—a tingling ran under my skin from my fingertips to my head. The poem was a star in my hand, lighting up the room. But I was a kid. I didn't know the power of it. I buried it in the depths of me like a dream deferred till it was real. For now, I searched for other paths of happiness.

….

My mom went to work one day and spoke to her friend, Claudette, about her goals.

"I need a home for me and my sons; they need their own space. And they need a father figure in their lives. I really need a new job, too, to make some more money," my mom said.

"Write it down. It will all come to you if you write it down and put it out in the universe," Claudette uttered.

My mom wrote it all down when she got home.

Soon after, my mom got a new job making more money doing purchasing at a place called Wellington in Paterson, NJ. Claudette told my mom about an apartment in Newark that was within my mom's new budget. My mom couldn't afford Summit. So, she moved us out of my grandmother's house in the green suburbs to a two-bedroom apartment in the cold, cracked pavement of Newark.

Shortly after moving into the apartment, my mom was putting up new curtains on the windows in the living room when she fell and broke her arm. She was home alone; my brothers and I had no idea. She got up and walked to the hospital about half a mile away, holding her arm.

We all sat in the living room and waited for her to come home. She entered the front door holding her arm with a white towel over it.

"Mom, what happened to your arm? Can I see?" I said approaching her.

"I fell. Look," she said lifting the towel.

There were metal rods of about four inches going into her arm. I was aghast and opened my mouth in shock. It was like Edward Scissorhands.

"Are you okay, Mommy?" I asked looking into her eyes. It was the first time I really felt bad for my mom, like I didn't want her to feel this pain.

"I'm okay," she said assuring us.

Aunt Yvonne called my mom on the phone.

"Hey Evelyn, how you doing?" she asked.

"I'm okay," my mom said.

"Well, I guess you'll be moving back into Mom's house?" Aunt Yvonne asked.

"No, I will be okay. I'm going to keep doing what's best for my family," she said.

Every day, my mom made sure we kept going to school in Summit. We woke up early to rush and get dressed for school in the clothes my mom bought us from the local flea market and my favorite British

Knights sneakers. I kept my mouth shut, embarrassed by my teeth covered with braces. Cory drove us to school in Summit in his car with no heat and the floor falling out, driving down the grimy roads of Newark. We passed our favorite corner store where we bought penny candy to sell, a barber shop to cut our high boxy hair, and sidewalks of trash and glass. We knew we were in Summit immediately after getting off the highway: the skies opened, the sun shined brighter, the air was crisp, and the roads were clean. The lives of people seemed better than ours. Parents smiled at their children in their massive homes. The windows were covered with white, lacey curtains showing antique furniture and a dog barking inside. I wanted to have that, to reach out and touch it.

After school, I played basketball in Grandma's backyard with my friends from Jefferson: a tall, light-skinned kid named Raheem, a short Costa Rican named Pablo, and my other friend Larry. Larry and I spent almost every day together since we were children, at school, after school at Grandma's, and at his house right behind Grandma's.

As we played, Mom yelled, "Tony, let's go!"

They looked at me confused.

"Why? I thought you lived here," they inquired.

I couldn't tell them we lived in Newark. Mom said we may get kicked out of school if Summit schools found out.

Once home, Mom kept us close to our apartment, hollering at us to come inside before the streetlights came on, and to not go further than a block away. Because of that, I guess I never really experienced any of the drug dealing, killings, and harshness of Newark I heard about. Tyrone, Cory, and I usually played video games or watched movies in Cory's room. I occasionally went outside with my friend, doing karate moves or backflips on mattresses in abandoned lots and running from the neighborhood gang of dogs. Back inside the apartment, my mom made me peanut butter sandwiches and cheeseburgers. She asked us to take out the trash while she cleaned up the kitchen and got ready for work the next day.

"Make sure y'all finish your homework," she said before we went back to our rooms.

"Yes, Ma," we answered, recalling the yelling we'd hear when our report card was bad.

"Did you take out the trash and clean your room like I said?"

"No, not yet," we replied with our usual response.

"Don't play those games till you do what I tell you to do," she said with her voice raising. Mom walked away exasperated.

…

One day, a guy came into the apartment with Mom. She introduced us.

"This is Norman. We work together at Wellington."

He smiled with a full gray beard and reached out to shake our hands. Tyrone and I looked at each other with the same scowl and walked away. I didn't like any minutes he spent in the apartment with us and our mom. We sat at the dinner table eating our cheeseburgers as he told us about his singing.

"You know, I was in the singing group Maurice Williams and The Zodiacs. We sang that song "Stay.[4]" It was in the movie *Dirty Dancing,*[5]" he said.

None of us said anything. I tried to ignore most of what he said, though it seemed interesting. I'd watched Dirty Dancing a few times and knew that part in the movie. We also didn't know anyone who used to be in a singing group. But none of this changed how I felt about him; he was here sitting next to my mother and wanted to be with her. Later, he told me to, "Take out the trash," holding the bag in his hand to give to me. I rolled my eyes and walked away. That summed up our

---

4   5

relationship. *Only my mother tells me what to do. You're not my father.*

It went on like that for years. Day after day it was Norman and Mom at the dinner table, Norman and Mom driving in the car, Norman asking me to take out the trash though I didn't listen to him. As Norman spent more time with us, I held onto a memory I had with my own father that played like a dream: my father and I walked down the street holding hands as he took me to the barbershop for a haircut. He patted me on my head as I looked up into his face blinded by the sun. Maybe it was a dream.

I gradually stopped seeing my father—once a week, once a month, until months went by, then years. It became us and Mommy. I didn't know why my father wasn't there. As a child, I didn't ask many questions. I'd gotten used to the life Mom built with us. Now, a new man was here, and I had no idea what to do with him as I was also growing up and dealing with my own view of the world.

Norman moved out of his one-bedroom apartment into our apartment, and I was forced to learn more about him. We went to North Carolina to visit Norman's family. We drove down a dirt road to the wooden home he grew up in, which leaned to one side and looked like it was built by hand with two bedrooms. His cousin's house was behind it, a single-level home with three bedrooms where we and his cousin's family slept. Norman introduced us, "These are my sons, Tony and Tyrone." But we continued to call him "Norman" the entire trip.

Back at home, Norman bought me a scooter and Tyrone a bike that we rode around on all day outside our apartment building. When we came inside, he asked us to take out the trash. I did what he said, but I cursed him under my breath. He was still just a man my mom was with that told me what to do. I didn't know whether he loved me or how I could love him. We needed more time.

When the wedding came around, my mom was fulfilling her list of goals. She came down the aisle in a blinding white dress looking like an angel in the church next to Grandma's house that we grew up going to. It was the prettiest I'd ever seen her. Norman was there at the altar, next to her with his full beard and tuxedo. The photos afterward captured how I felt. My mouth was shut, unable to smile, as I lined up next to my brothers and Mom. I only felt better when Michael Jackson came on. I was able to dance in my slippery dress shoes next to my uncle Greg who was the king of dancing in our family.

After the wedding ceremony and reception, we all came home, and Mom put her wedding dress away. She immediately went back to work. There was no honeymoon, no time to relax. Moving to Summit was on her mind.

One day, we all came home to the apartment door open. When we walked into the living room, the TV and radio were gone. The wires were still dangling from the wall behind the TV stand. We all shook our heads and stared at the sight, almost not believing we were in such a situation.

The next day, Tyrone and I armed ourselves with a kitchen knife and bat and waited in the apartment for the robber to come back. When we heard the wind blow, we gave each other a look that said *he's back*, dropped our weapons, and climbed out of our second-floor window. A couple weeks later, we went to a neighbor's apartment across the hall and noticed they had a new TV and VCR that looked just like ours. All of us looked at each other as we left their apartment, meeting each other's eyes with the same look. It was time to move.

Around that time, Mom got a raise at her job, becoming a manager at Wellington Patio Furniture. Norman had good credit. They reached out to a real estate agent in Summit who found a house for rent. My mom didn't look at any other houses; she knew this was for us. Our family was ready to live where they'd always wished to be, to show our family wealth and what Black kids could achieve in Summit.

New Me

Moving to Summit was a new life. My eyes lit up as we pulled into the driveway of our new home in Summit, leaving behind years of living in Newark. The sun shone on our yellow house on the tree-lined street. The home was a perfect square with two windows and shutters on the top floor, a bay window on the bottom above the bushes, and the front door was an entrance to new memories. The thought of the two-bedroom apartment we had just left faded as we walked in. The neighborhood was still and quiet with birds chirping; it was waiting for us to make noise.

We ran upstairs to see the bedrooms: Mom and Norman had their own bedroom with their own bathroom inside it. I'd never seen that before. There was another bathroom in the hallway for us brothers to use. Cory had his own room next to ours, which was much better than living in the living room of our last apartment. He moved his furniture into his room then headed to work in his sporty Trans Am car that Norman helped him buy.

Ty and I went in our room where our beds didn't nearly touch each other. Our windows looked out onto the street with views of the neighborhood—the brown brick Tudor house across the street with a golf course behind it.

Down the stairs, the living room and dining room were fit for parties. We could finally put a TV to watch *A Different World*, showing Black kids in college, and listen to Bob Marley and my mom's CDs on our new five-disc CD player. We could leave the front door unlocked without any worries of any of it getting stolen. We put a pool table in the basement, just like at Grandma's. But it wasn't Grandma's; this house was all ours.

I took a walk up and down the street looking at the homes and neighbors; we were the only Black people in the neighborhood.

In the morning, I got dressed and got a ride to my new school, Summit Middle School. I smiled widely to all the new kids, showing my white teeth without braces. I was no longer embarrassed and beamed with joy I'd hidden for years. Kids from all over town ran around outside near the parking lot: predominately White kids with a small number of Black, Asian, and Hispanic. There were a lot of cute, White girls. Mom said I can love who I want, and that love was color blind.

I ran around inside the white halls with bright lights, orange metal lockers, sneakers squeaking and stomping on the floors, and posters flinging off the walls from the scuttle and wind.

In gym class, kids threw the dodgeball with all their might, hurling lightning at other kids' heads. Then I carried that energy down the halls to Math and English class with classmates. In chorus, the teacher made me sing in a deep baritone voice, ruining my chances of being Michael Jackson. After class, I followed cute girls in the hallways. A few of the other boys and I pinched the girls' butts and ran away, giggling. After school, I hung with my normal crew, the ones I grew up with and went to elementary school with. Larry and I looked the same with our flat top hair like Kid and Play and wore our clothes backwards like Kris Kross. Usually, we'd head down the hill next to Grandma's house to play basketball at the community recreational center, trying to dunk on the lower rims or dribble past each other.

But that day, I noticed a group of kids who were heading home from school with pale skin, blond and brown hair, button-down shirts, khaki shorts, and backpacks with their initials. A couple of them spun poles with circular nets on one end—lacrosse sticks. I'd never even seen these sticks before. My friends and I started making fun of the kids for their sticks, backpacks, and the way they looked wearing button-down Polo shirts. One of my friends had a ball and tried to hit one of the kids, Chris, with it. Chris smirked with a crooked smile as he blocked the ball with his lacrosse stick. My laughter faded as I thought *that was cool.* Maybe they shouldn't be made fun of; maybe they were just different.

My friends and I headed away to the parking lot on our way to hang out. Some days we'd slipped cans of soda and candy bars in our coats, stealing from a local store down the block or jump over the fence of the community pool, sneaking in a swim. We used one of Raheem's BB guns to shoot out traffic lights on Mischief Night, the night before Halloween.

But I turned back to look at that group of kids with the backpacks and lacrosse sticks heading to the big homes in the hills behind the school.

"T!" my friends shouted, calling for me to come.

I looked back at the kids heading to the hills again. *What are their lives like?* I wondered. I wanted to experience something different, the lifestyle my mom wanted us Black kids to experience in Summit.

…

I was in gym class playing basketball with a kid named Jamie. He played just as hard or even harder than me, grabbing rebounds and dribbling. After gym, Jamie came up to me smiling and asked if I wanted to come to his house after school to hang out. Later, I met up with him, a short kid named Andrew who everyone called Coop, a skinny blond-haired kid named Keith, and Chris. Girls were in skirts with sticks having field hockey practice behind the school as we walked a few blocks to the homes on the hill. I kept my astonishment to myself as my head turned from side to side seeing the houses get bigger and bigger.

I arrived at Jamie's house. It was seemingly twice the size of mine, where a basketball hoop was at the end of the driveway and soccer and lacrosse nets were in the backyard.

We went inside his home filled with family photos of his mom, dad, and brothers smiling brightly and hugging each other. I moved throughout the house noticing a fireplace, nautical designs, deep blue couches, high ceilings, wooden, antique-like furniture, a nook area off the kitchen, and the kitchen overlooking the living room. It was like traveling to a new land, and it was foreign to me. I was learning about a new culture and new people.

I initially jumped at the sight of Jamie's big dog, a chocolate Labrador wagging her tail so hard it banged into the furniture. I used to run from dogs in Newark. One bit my cousin Steve in the face and another growled at me at Grandma's, but this one was gleeful. It was part of what some dreamed of: a big home, family, and a dog. The white picket fence was unnecessary to see how fortunate they were.

Jamie opened his fridge to get us some Gatorades, and we grabbed homemade rice krispy treats and cookies on the way to the basement. I wanted more than my hands could carry, but everyone else acted like this was normal, running down the basement stairs without a thought.

They moved like brothers with each other, comfortable in their relationship that I had just entered. They spit words like "dude" and cursed. I laughed as they laughed around the room of wood-paneled walls, hockey sticks leaning against them, a stack of lacrosse sticks in the corner, a gaming system under the TV with stereo and speakers on either side blasting guitar music.

Jamie said, "There's other music besides hip hop." He grinned as he put on the <u>Dave Matthews Band.</u>[6] I was a little hurt that he would belittle my music like that. But I opened my ears and listened to the words and guitar playing, smirking at this new music that tickled my eardrums.

Jamie grabbed a couple of lacrosse sticks and golf clubs, and we headed to the backyard where he showed me how to hold the lacrosse stick with two hands, rocking the ball, and shooting. Keith showed the wrapping of my fingers around the golf club with a swing. I knew I couldn't play any of these sports for the school because of my heart murmur, but I continued wanting to play them here with my new friends.

Soon after, we rode our bikes up to Keith's house; we pulled up out of breath. It was bigger than Jamie's and seemed grander being on the highest hills in

6

town, as if these homes and lives were better than those below them.

Keith's mom beamed and shook my hand, welcoming me. She was bright like the sun and her eyes seemed to have no worries, only kindness.

"Hi Tony," she said in a gentle whisper.

"Hi, Mrs. Morano," I responded with a smile and kind tone, showing respect using only her last name, something Ma and Grandma taught me.

Me and the boys balled like at Grandma's. Jamie was overly athletic, grabbing most rebounds, driving to the hoop, and making most of his shots. Chris was kinda crazy; he couldn't shoot well but he somehow got rebounds and launched a terrible shot over the backboard. Coop was my height and played like me, usually crossing over then taking it in for a layup.

Keith's blond hair flopped as he dribbled. He continuously talked shit too, called us to guard him then make this far away shot. "In your face, you suck." Coop and I hated it and would look at each other to plan to foul Keith hard, balling our fists. But we knew we weren't going to do anything. I'd never been in a fight, and no one wanted to hurt Keith. Besides, it was funny, so we laughed about it and accepted it was how Keith was.

I was surrounded by these kids and their smiling faces. They were new friends showing me who they were. I was accepting them as they accepted me. Deep down, as the minutes ticked by, I wanted someone to share these early teenager times with, while not knowing exactly why they wanted me there. In the words that passed between us, never did they once mention the color of my skin. I hoped they wouldn't. I looked away as they looked at me waiting for what I was going to say next. I felt compelled to put my blackness away as I was being fed this new life, challenging me to change my view of myself and other people. It made me feel different, like someone else outside of being a Black boy. I was a boy, like them, talking about girls' butts, what happened in class, and how to kick a soccer ball. I wanted more of it.

After hours of playing around, the evening was here. Keith's dad pulled into the driveway driving one of those luxury cars I used to wish were mine as a kid. He said hi with a stern look, square chin, and a height that overshadowed us. I looked at him in his business clothes, pulling a suitcase, and hunched back knowing he worked hard all day for what they had. Keith said he hadn't seen him in days because he was on a business trip. His eyes were red. I didn't know if he was angry or tired, so it scared me. But he did smile. Keith's mother and father were there. They were a family, and I wasn't used to seeing this. The streetlights came on, and Keith's parents said it was time to go; he had to do his homework. *I have to get home too.*

When I got to my house, Mom sat at the dining room table, working on printed out spreadsheets and paying bills. She reminded me to do my homework as I sat down beside her and pulled out my books.

On the weekend, my family headed down to Grandma's house. Aunts and uncles and cousins brought food and we ate around the dining room table. Afterward, Grandma brought out a few white envelopes as my cousin, Aman, and some others stood up in a row in front of her. She told them how proud she was that they were graduating high school and going to college. She handed them the envelopes filled with money. They smiled and blushed.

Aman pulled out a hundred dollars from the envelope. It was small compared to thousands of dollars for college tuition, but it was the most money I'd ever seen my grandmother give anyone. Aman gripped the dollar bills as I looked up to him from my seat, recalling his days of crushing guys on the football field with Tyrone and tossing the ball on the lacrosse field with some of his friends, most of whom didn't need the one hundred dollars. Now he was off to Boston for college with the help of financial aid.

The smiles of my mom, aunts, uncles, and grandparents who didn't go to college widened. Aunt Jeanette, Aman's mother, grinned like the other single moms in the room, including my mother and Aunt Esther. They were looking towards this next generation to carry on what they didn't do. They were proud. I held on to that.

I saw myself on the right path. I was going to get the best grades and go to the best college in my family, for my family. It was the first time I was deciding who I wanted to become.

…

It was all part of the new world.

I stood next to Keith and Coop outside school near the parking lot as a girl, Jennifer, with blonde hair, peachy skin, glasses, and a round butt wrapped her arms around me and shoved her tongue down my throat like she'd done it many times before. We met like many other boys and girls meet; we'd seen each other in homeroom. She gave me her number on a piece of paper, and we called each other on our home phones. But this was my first kiss; my lips smooshed against her pink lips. My eyes opened looking at her face pressed against mine. I was unable to believe what was happening yet trying to go along with it, moving my tongue around hers and outside of her mouth. It was over just as fast as it started. My new friends laughed with me.

I was invited to a B'nei mitzvah for twins, Lindsay and Terry, who had the same birthday as me. I never heard of such an event. I was astonished by the shiny black and white invitation. Mom bought me a nice suit and I went. I was the only Black boy there and danced the electric slide in my white suit jacket while Keith and Coop cheered me on in their blue blazers and khakis.

Coop showed me how to play tennis at Memorial Field, whipping the ball at me as I chased it to lob it back to him with my racket. Later, I went to his house for a sleepover. His home was sprawling—all white outside and inside, which seemed stark yet elegant. His mom, who kindly welcomed me, had striking blue eyes and stringy blonde hair. His dad approached wearing glasses and a had a sort of quirkiness about him.

His older and younger sister were all there making jokes about one another and cursing. Coop laughed like a chipmunk, but at school he usually shoved nerds who wore glasses into the lockers. He ended up in fights like the time he punched this kid with six toes in the face. I rooted for Coop as my friend, but deep down I sympathized with the other boy for being different.

Before dinner, Coop said, "Shit, mom, what are we having for dinner?"

"I don't know. Probably pancakes," Coop's mom said.

"Fucking pancakes?" Coop responded. I laughed. It was hilarious, but inside I was shocked. I hardly said "damn" in front of my mom. We went up to his room, and he had bunk beds which reminded me of my room at Grandma's. I grabbed the top bunk as he yelled at his younger sister for coming in his room, and we laughed ourselves to sleep. We had to get up early because Coop had to go to church.

Back at school, posters were on the wall and announcements were made about the school dance coming up that weekend. The boys and I talked about the girls who were going to be there and how we couldn't wait. When it came time, we met each other in the gym. The DJ turned on early 90s[7] music; the speakers bumped as we jumped to "Jump" by Kris Kross and we grinded our crotches up against girls when "Rump Shaker" by Wreckx N Effect came on. A few Black girls danced by twisting their legs and hips to the house music song "Follow Me." Jamie tried to do the running man dance that I taught him, his feet sliding then skipping. Keith and I recited the words to "Scenario" by Tribe Called Quest; I always tried to say Busta Rhymes' part. When the song "End of the Road" by Boyz II Men came on, I looked for my friend Lindsay. I put my hands on her hips to slow dance, remembering this was our favorite song as we lip-synced the words.

On most of my other days, I rode my bike up all the hills of Summit to Keith's house. We were chilling in his basement, flipping through his stacks of CDs to pick out the best hip hop. I was amazed by his collection; I ran my hands across the circular discs of Tribe Called Quest and others. I saw music from Black people I had

7

never heard of, and I wondered if he knew more about hip hop than I did. He asked me, "Have you heard this CD? Have you heard this song?" A lot of the time, I didn't know. I wondered if I should know more of this as a Black kid; I didn't see him ask Jamie and Coop these questions. But he showed me the music anyway. We listened to melodic beats and rhymes from the music on his stereo while playing video games, clicking buttons on the controllers. We did this almost every day—sitting side by side on the couch.

On that couch, Keith told me he wanted to go to a good college to make his parents proud. He felt the pressure to do well. Keith's eyes twinkled and his shoulders were tight like he meant it, and he was carrying that weight. Keith's oldest brother, Joe, was a giant like my brother Cory. But I heard Joe passed away from a drug overdose at a young age. I couldn't bring it up to Keith at this moment; I didn't know what to say or how to handle such pain. Keith's older brother, Brad, was going in a similar path and didn't do well in school.

I recalled Cory didn't go to college and Tyrone also didn't get good grades. Keith and I were in similar classes; when we got our tests back, he showed me his higher grade, which made me want to do better.

Keith came over my house to sleep over. Before stepping through the front door, I was a little ashamed my house was so much smaller than his. But Keith came in to say hi to my mom, put on some hip hop in our CD player, ate some of my mom's food, and then slept on our green leather couch. In his home, the size and decorations were different than my home. He had a pool in the backyard with a shiny car in the driveway. Yet, we connected.

Time went by. I was talking to my new girlfriend, Olivia, in the school parking lot. She smiled up at me with thin lips on her petite body as her wavy blonde hair glistened. I gazed into her eyes through her glasses as we held hands and giggled next to Keith, Jennifer, and some other friends. She had a ski tag on her brightly colored jacket and told me she was going on the school's ski trip that weekend.

"Ok. I'll talk to you when you get back." I smiled as we parted.

On Monday, back at school, I didn't hear from Olivia. I didn't see her before school as I stood near the parking lot. She wasn't in the hallways. I didn't get a call at home last night and talk to her, like we used to when she gave me her number. Our relationship started just a few weeks ago; it was weird now.

I walked into the cafeteria and sat next to Keith at a table with some of the other guys. I watched a table across the room where Olivia sat laughing with her friends.

Keith leaned in and whispered, "Yo, Olivia hooked up with Ned over the weekend at the ski trip."

I was immediately crushed. I wondered how the ski trip was. I pictured Olivia and her friends in their ski jackets sliding along down the hill in their skis, planting poles in the snow as their hair flowed through the cold air. I didn't really know how it was because I never skied before.

My eyes burned while watching Olivia across the cafeteria. The noise of kids' laughter and talking usually echoed, but in this moment, I heard nothing. I only heard her laughing with her friends; her wavy blonde hair bouncing, and her chatting like nothing was wrong.

I looked at Keith and said, "Thanks for telling me."

After school, I met up with Olivia near the parking lot. We walked over to a quiet area where the other kids couldn't see us behind the bushes. We held hands as I looked down at her blue eyes and wide smile through her braces. My face was straight, trying to remain calm.

"I heard you hooked up with Ned," I said.

Her cheeriness faded in the cool air, and we let go of hands. "Yeah," she looked away.

Rage boiled up inside of me and I stormed off, stomping down the hill to my grandmother's house.

Sitting on the back porch, still huffing and fighting back tears, my grandmother came out and sat next to me. If I were a child, she'd probably ask me for a kiss: "Come give grandma some sugar." But right now, I saw her out of the corner of my eye looking down at me wrapped in her smooth, chocolate skin. I sensed her warm glow.

"Boy, what's wrong with you? Sitting there with your mouth poked out," she said.

"My girlfriend cheated on me," I muffled.

"Shouldn't have been messing with those fast girls anyway," she said.

I laughed inside by the twang and words from the South that only my grandma says. Within minutes, I was forgetting about the event with my girlfriend and thought about my friend Keith telling me. He looked out for me.

Soon after, Keith and I were in Spanish class in the back of the room laughing as the teacher spoke. The door to the classroom opened and the vice principal told the teacher to send me to her office after class. The teacher nodded and looked at me while Keith and I froze. My heart nearly fell out of my chest. *What did I do wrong?* The laughing between us ceased.

Outside of her office, she pulled me aside. "Tony, I've been speaking to some of your teachers. We noticed you've been doing really well in your classes. And we think you need to be challenged more. What do you think of going to the private school, Newark Academy? We'd help your mom pay for it, of course."

"Newark Academy?" I asked looking at her.

"Yes, it will be really good for you," she replied.

At that moment, Keith ran past us and gave me a joking look, smiled, and made silly faces that made me laugh. I knew the answer.

"No. I don't want to go," I told her.

Fresh Men

I was a freshman at Summit High School in 1993. I went to school listening to my <u>Tribe Called Quest CD</u>[8] on my CD player, wearing baggy jeans, Timberland boots, and a plaid flannel from Britches that looked like Polo but was cheaper. A few hundred kids swarmed the school's entry doors and hallways; only a few handfuls of Black and other ethnicities. Younger kids were dropped off by their parents or walked to school, while the older kids drove their Volkswagen Jettas or Ford Explorers to the school parking lot. Blonde-haired girls with bangs walked into the school wearing colorful sweaters and beaded necklaces. Other kids were in marron and white Varsity sports jackets, with an embroidered "S" for Summit. Small groups of

8

kids wore braided hair and the baggiest clothes below their waist. It was like scenes out of the show *90210*.

Keith, Coop, and I were little men in a new world of people who have been at this school longer than us, and who were older and bigger than us. We tried not to cower as freshmen. Then we'd see our siblings. Coop's older sister walked by and would nudge him or call him a nerd and they'd laugh. Jamie's older brother, Cassidy, gave him a head nod. Keith's older brother, Brad, hung with guys that would punch you in the face if you looked at them wrong. Brad freaked me out since the time we all shoveled the snow in Keith's driveway, and he only wore shorts with no shirt on, and said, "Pain is in the mind" with blood shot eyes. Keith was small, but we all knew no one would mess with him because of Brad's protection.

Tyrone and his buddies walked down the hallways, filled the spaces with their echoing voices and were almost twice the size of us with their football jerseys on. The teachers gave them high-fives and laughed with them as if they owned the school. We saw them come our way.

"Hey, Tyrone's little brother," they'd say and chuckle at me.

I grinned at them and my brother with adoration. Everyone knew my brother; he was a star football player. Everyone said hi to him and he went to all the parties, including the ones at the biggest and richest houses. He always had a cute girlfriend, like the most popular girl in school named Brenda or this other girl, Corina, that played a guitar and sang like Jewel.

After school and on the weekends, my friends and I went to Keith's house, what we now called Club Morano's, like the popular Club Med. We waved hi to Keith's cheery mom, ran down to the basement where Keith put on his music, and we played NHL and Madden NFL on the Sega video game system. Keith would let everyone know he was the best at the games, talking shit, and making Coop mad. I didn't mind always losing; I enjoyed our time together.

When it was hot, we hopped in Keith's pool and played pool basketball which was almost as competitive as our regular basketball. Jamie jumped out of the water to grab the ball, and Coop and I went in for layups. Keith had this new trick where he'd call me to guard him then cough up a loogy of mucus, spit it on my arm, and score while I froze in disgust.

Afterwards, we'd grab snacks and drinks and continue to relax. We'd sometimes order pizza from Joe's hoping my brother Cory would deliver. I couldn't wait to show Keith and my friends that I had an older brother with a cool car and worked at our favorite place. I was proud of my brother, even though he couldn't afford to go to college and delivered pizza as a side job.

We were all around sixteen years old, so times began to change; we were drinking alcohol now. An older kid from Keith's golf team knocked on Keith's back door near the basement and gave us beer to drink, usually a case of the cheapest he could get from a liquor store in Newark where they didn't check IDs. We were lightweight drinkers, amateurs. We slowly drank three

Bud Light Ice beers or wine coolers which went down our throats like broken glass. We'd wobble when we walked, our speech was slurry, and vision blurry just after a few drinks. We didn't have anything else to do living in the suburbs. We were also just being introduced to the issues with underage drinking.

One night, I was walking down the street with Coop and some other friends, and the cops pulled up to us. I wasn't drinking or doing anything wrong, so I waited to hear what they had to say. They asked Coop to open his backpack on the hood of their cop car. Bottles of Zima rolled onto the hood and fell to the street. I froze. I was ashamed, not only because we got caught, but because Zima was the weakest drink, and people would make fun of us for drinking it. They put us in the police car and brought us to the police station. Coop's dad came into the police station with a burning red face. He was livid! I went home alone, unscathed, because I was innocent and did nothing wrong.

...

As I entered the school for Sophomore year, my stride had more confidence. I headed straight to my lockers to see Keith and my other buddies. We laughed while grabbing our books, teachers yelling at us not to run in the hallways as we headed off to class. In class, Keith whispered jokes to get Coop to laugh out loud, and Coop would call some girl fat or throw something, getting him kicked out. Then I'd hear Coop cackling with someone as I went to my next class. In between classes, kids hung outside on the side of the school, smoking cigarettes away from the sight of teachers. I'd go out in the front with Coop and others to kick a hacky sack or just joke around. Coop seemed to always be in the hallways.

After school, I watched as Keith went to golf practice and Coop, Jamie, and Chris went off to lacrosse practice. I imagined going somewhere to play a sport too. But I couldn't because of my heart murmur. I went back into the school to go to my singing practice for an upcoming event with the mayor.

I said "Hey," and gave high-fives to the other two guys wearing glasses, and we began.

As my voice bellowed, I continued thinking how uncool this was and how my friends were playing sports.

Later, I went to the doctor's office to check on the results from my latest physical exam. I gripped my knees while sitting on the doctor's chair waiting in anticipation.

The doctor entered in his white coat, looking over a few papers in his hand.

"You can play sports now. It looks like your heart murmur is gone," the doctor said.

I nearly jumped at the news. The disappointment from years and years of not being able to play sports at school and having received bad news from this doctor was finally going away and being replaced with an open door of possibilities in my latter teen years. I was filled with choices as I left the office. I immediately thought of basketball. *I can finally play for the school.*

When I got to gym class, I did the most pull ups and lifted the most weight, trying to be strong like my brothers and stronger than the skinny me that was made fun of. And when it was time for the fifty-yard dash, I tried to fly away as my feet hardly touched the ground while running as fast as I could, faster than anyone in the class. The gym teacher told me about track and field and said I'd be good.

After school, I went down to the field for practice with the rest of the team: speeding around the track, flying in the long jump, going up and over in the high jump. I was out of breath at the end of practice, but I also was bored. Running was monotonous, and there was no change in direction. I wanted to pass a team member a ball and score points. I knew I wanted to do something else.

I walked up to another field where Coop, Jamie, and Chris were having lacrosse practice. They twirled their sticks, flung the ball to each other, and ran from one end to the other. When they finished, they ran over to me.

"I'm just checking you guys out. Maybe I'll join," I said jokingly.

"Yeah, you should definitely join the team, Tony."

They called over the coach who was like a bear, seemingly eight feet tall, broad chest, wide shoulders, and thick neck. He twirled a lacrosse stick, comparatively, as small as a toothpick in his paw like hands.

I looked at my friends and the other team members and didn't see any other Black kids. And it encouraged me. I didn't want to be like other Black kids who were expected to play basketball. I saw the school's basketball team with mostly Black kids, recalled playing basketball at Grandma's growing up, and watching basketball on TV with mostly Black players. I remembered driving through Newark and other towns where Black kids played on hoops with no nets, and Black kids scored the most points. I didn't see Black people playing many other sports other than basketball and football. I considered my height. *I'm not tall enough to be that great at basketball. But I can be one of the fastest kids here.*

I already felt different—this wasn't just about playing a sport. I felt it deep down, from wanting to dance in front of my family to writing my poem about molded cheese to my new friends and the path to college. They were all decisions I made. This was part of me changing and defining myself.

My mom said I can do anything. I can do this. Black people can do other things . . .

"I don't know how to play or have any equipment or anything." I told him, looking down and feeling ashamed.

"That's okay. We have equipment. We can get you some of the other things. Come down tomorrow." Coach said.

"I got a stick and some other equipment," Chris said.

"Okay," I said.

I went home and told my mom. She looked understandably confused; she didn't know anything about lacrosse. "Okay. What you need?"

I knew we couldn't afford much. I told her I just needed cleats, and I could get the rest from my friends and the team. She took me to a sports store and got me my first pair of cleats. I felt like a new person as soon as I put them on.

I walked down to the field after school. I was a wreck the first few practices: the helmet loosely twisted around my head, guys flung the ball at me and hit me in the face, then they ran at me, crushing me to the ground as I tried to pick up the ball. My feet ached from wearing cleats for the first time. I held Chris's lacrosse stick that he lent me and practiced catching and cradling the ball.

Coach told me, "Tony, you clear the ball." I nodded and knew I had to get the ball to the other side of the field. That's why I was there. I heard a friend on the team say, "See the color of his skin; he's going to run fast."

I put that behind me and put everything I had into my feet, running the ball down the sideline, almost a hundred yards, leaving the defense behind me to my team's offense in front of me. I was the fastest kid on the team. When I passed it to Jamie, I got hit and went flying, spinning like a helicopter. I got up in a cloud of dust completely out of breath. I saw Jamie and the team celebrating as we scored. I wanted to lie down but Coach said stay in, so I dragged myself around the field out of breath.

After, we huddled closely, arms wrapped around each other's shoulders in a circle, like a family at dinner. The coach told us all it was a good game. I was feeling confident, and I felt like I contributed something to that with every inch of my body. I was lucky to only have to walk a few blocks home from the field, as my legs and arms were tired. No parents or anyone else was going to pick me up. This sport was all my choice, my responsibility, and for me. The sport was now a part of me.

. . .

Every day, I was busy playing sports after school and doing homework, but weekends were still mine to hang out and enjoy time with my friends. Before going anywhere, Mom made sure Tyrone and I helped around the house by cleaning up before company came over— shampooing the rugs, painting our rooms white for like the twentieth time, putting up wallpaper, and helping Norman with his garage sale, selling patio furniture items from their job. Then I got dressed and ran out the house.

Now that my friends and I were slightly older, our drinking continued to increase. We showed up drunk at a sweet sixteen party at the American Legion club and sloppily kissed girls while dancing. We guzzled alcohol and went to dances at private all-girls schools like Oak Knoll where Chris's girlfriend went. But the best times were house parties when my friends' parents weren't home.

We still snuck beers down into Keith's basement. But we quickly downed four to six beers. We were drinking forty ounces of Old English malt liquor like hip hop artists drank in music videos. We listened to <u>rap</u>[9] like "<u>C.R.E.A.M.</u>," "<u>Protect Ya Neck</u>" by Wu-Tang, and "<u>Regulator</u>" by Warren G. When we rapped the songs, we skipped over saying "nigger" in the lyrics. We all knew we shouldn't say it. "<u>Juicy</u>" by Notorious BIG came on and we all sang: "It was all a dream, I used to read Word Up! magazine."

Keith, Coop, and I met up with Chris and a few others to walk over to a party at a friend's house. Normally, I would be the designated driver. I was the oldest and the only one who had their driver's license. I was grateful for Chris's mom who paid for my driving lessons and watched me fail the driving test three times!

But she lent me their long station wagon to drive him and my friends around.

But that night, we knew we all were drinking, so I wasn't driving. The house party was filled with other guys and girls from our school. I stood with my friends and my cousin, Hakim, who'd also started hanging with us. Though Hakim was a year younger than us, he was bigger than us. Everyone expected him to play football, but he didn't play any sports for school. He also dated a girl older than us and knew all our friends. Hakim and I were similar; we both grew up together with little money. His best friends were White and standing next to him just like mine. We were usually the only Black kids at parties, this being one of those cases. And we were both smiling and enjoying our time together. It was like we were still kids at Grandma's house.

Hakim pulled out some marijuana that looked like dried dirt, branches, and leaves. He crumbled it in his large hands, delicately rolled it into a joint in white paper, and licked and sealed it. Then he put it on the end of a TV antenna. It resembled a pipe—a long, thin, silver, hollow rod about a foot long. It was magic; he was MacGyver. I was amazed as I stood there with a beer, thinking he was so much cooler than I was. He'd obviously done this before as him and his friends got ready to smoke it. This was unknown to me; it was illegal to smoke weed.

However, I sucked on the metal as thick smoke and what seemed like thorns entered my throat. I coughed so hard I thought I would cough up blood and a lung along with all my air. Then we laughed and joked as we passed it around, and I toked on it, puff after puff. I then saw Hakim dig a hole out of an apple and put weed in it and lighting it up. He was a mad scientist with the weed.

But after smoking the apple and having clouds form around my head, my vision of the girls laughing and guys playing beer games got more and more blurred. Moments later, I opened my eyes to find myself sitting in a chair in a garage where my friend, Ann, was putting ice on my ear and sticking a needle through it, piercing it. I laughed so hard my stomach ached. Fortunately, no cops showed up to break up the party. I'd probably stumble and fall on my face if I tried to run fast. The party ended and we went home. I woke up on Keith's couch, groggy with empty microwave pizza boxes and beer cans around. We cleaned up and I headed home. The following weekend we'd hang out and do it all over again. I was loving it.

...

A few weeks later, I was in the cafeteria, usually eating my rectangular pizza and waiting for a possible food fight. Someone yelled, "There's a fight in the parking lot! Tony, Tyrone is going to fight."

I jumped up and headed outside with the other kids. Someone called one of Tyrone's friends "nigger," and about twenty kids rushed out of the building, including my brother and his friends, and the other kid and his friends. It was immediate mayhem. Two kids squared up against each other as others jumped in. They threw punches in between the parked cars as other kids yelled and watched. I tried to stop it, stepping in between to ease and protect my brother and his friends. In the distance, someone took a bat out of their truck, and I froze. *No. He's going to hurt my brother.* As the kid swung the bat, my brother raised his arm and blocked it, waving it off as a brush of wind and kept fighting. He was a superhero.

On the weekends, my friends and I, and the rest of the town went to the high school football game at Tatlock Field to watch my brother continue his superhero abilities, crushing other players on the field with his team.

"Go, Tyrone!" I'd yell as everyone knew that was my brother, and I was proud of him.

Ty's team won the championship before, so a win seemed to light up the town. Norman sat in the stands not far from me and my friends, watching the game and telling people that was his son playing. He nor anyone else came to my lacrosse games; I knew these football games were more important. The music from the band played, drums banging with trumpets, and I'd go down and dance with some of my cheerleader friends. At halftime, we grabbed ice cream at Magic Fountain and came back to watch Tyrone tackle a few more guys until they won.

One night, Ty told me he was having a party at our house while Mom and Norman were out of town in Atlantic City. This was prime time for people to come over to party while our parents were gone and theirs were home. Ty said I could bring Keith. I spoke to Keith on the house phone and was running around the house excited to be at the party. Ty said, "It's only going to be a few people," but word of the party seemed to spread by Tyrone's popular girlfriend as unexpected people walked through the front door. Kids brought kegs of beer to the backyard and put them in garbage cans of ice along with bottles and bottles of liquor. I recognized all of Tyrone's friends from football by the stories he told me.

In our room, he'd tell me about parties at their house in the hills of Summit where their homes were so massive, he got lost in them. He joked that he drove down the driveway and thought it was a street. Some of their parents were the richest in town and in the state of New Jersey. He said one friend got drunk and crashed his forty-thousand-dollar car, a Nissan Pathfinder, and then his parents immediately bought him a new one. As Ty told me these stories, his eyes glimmered like he wanted a piece of what they had. Now they'd brought their lives into our home because of Tyrone.

Someone cooked food on our grill as music blasted in the backyard. The house was filled with people walking through our living room, dirtying the plastic runner protecting the floor, and sitting on our green leather sofas. Pool balls clang in the basement, people sat in our kitchen nook, and stood around talking in our backyard only a few feet away from neighbor's yards for them to hear and see.

Keith and I sipped a beer and giggled like we were so cool to be with older kids. Meanwhile, they occasionally made fun of me. "Tyrone's little brother, you can't drink." I was already buzzed.

The party went on like many other parties we went to. Keith and I attempted to chat with girls older than us, and everyone drank alcohol though we knew we weren't old enough.

I went out in the front yard and heard the music from the street as the cops pulled up. Party was over. One of the police officers asked Tyrone's friend to say his ABCs backwards and he responded, "You say your ABCs backwards," as they all laughed.

Later, my mom said she was fined for Tyrone's party. "The cops came to our house because we're Black," she told us. I looked at her in disbelief; I didn't want to think that.

It was the last time Ty had a party at the house, which meant the last time I had a party.

...

When the summer came, my mom told Tyrone and I that we could make a few dollars working with her and Norman at their job. I don't remember having much of a choice, but I knew we both wanted some money for the summer to hang out at the Summit Community Pool with our friends.

So, we spent our days getting up early with my mom. Norman drove us to their job in Paterson where the factory was. As my mom went up to her office, Ty and I followed Norman to the factory. He told us to "Move these boxes of patio cushions on the conveyor belt. Be careful when you press this button." We watched the boxes roll on the belt and we were giddy with such responsibility.

Norman took us on walks through the empty factory filled with dust and cobwebs, since production had slowed at this plant. He showed us how to move pallets of boxes with the pallet jacket. Sometimes Ty and I would be goofing off by karate kicking pieces of Styrofoam and Norman would come in and tell us to get back to work. We'd look at him and stop playing. It was one of the first times we obeyed him. This was unlike the earlier times back in Newark when we'd laugh when he'd say, "Take out the trash," which we've also gotten better at.

We knew Norman was proud of us being his family—from attending Tyrone's football games to teaching me how to drive manual stick shift to now when he walked us around the factory telling people we were his sons. We were in his place of work, respecting and almost admiring how he knew where everything was, how to operate the machines, and how people smiled when they said hi to him. We went back to the office where Mom would have lunch with us and show us her metal desk with a large computer monitor and stacks of paper on it. To us, she managed the company. Everyone came to her with questions, and she knew the answer.

At the end of the week, the company put out a "Patio Sale" sign, opened the parking lot gate, and customers would pull up their cars to buy patio umbrellas and chair cushions. Norman would turn to us and say, "Go get that umbrella and cushions out the back and bring it to her car." We'd do it, and the lady would give us a tip.

It went on like that throughout the summer. The boxes were getting fewer and fewer, emptying the factory, and people gave us more and more tips, filling our pockets with wads of cash. As we drove home, my brother and I counted the money that bulged in our pockets. For a second, I thought of spending it my own way to buy pizza, food, and hang out with Keith and my other friends. Yet, I thought of how Keith and others were on vacations or at the pool during the summer while I worked. I looked at my brother and realized the summer working with him was ending.

Soon after, I watched Ty bring a trunk into our room and pack up his things to go to college. He told me he was going to St Peter's University in Jersey City to play football. I watched a piece of me—my friend whom I shared a room with all my life—walk out the front door and get in the car to pursue his own path.

Sure, sometimes my brother made me mad. He stole my CD player, put me in a headlock at home, and said I couldn't fight. But deep down, I wondered how it would be if he wasn't there at school and at home with me. Who was I without him?

Lessons

Junior year started; there was a sense we were getting older with my brother gone and younger kids coming in. We began to realize school wasn't the most important thing in our lives. We were going to learn more about ourselves outside of the classroom. Luckily, my friends and I were handling these days together.

When I entered the school, I said hi to a few other kids including Larry and Raheem, who I hadn't really hung out with in a long time. I was with Keith and Coop and a couple of girls like Ann. Out of the corner of my eye, I caught a glimpse of a few Black girls: one I took to a school dance, one talking to them, and another with smooth chocolate skin, a bright white smile with luscious lips I'd love to kiss. Her eyes looked over at me, and she looked me up and down assessing my clothes and my friends. She rolled her eyes away in disgust while saying something to her friends. I tucked the sting of her look in my back pocket. I had an idea of what she said to her friends. I just didn't want to deal with the hurt right now. I had to get to class and focus on the most important year for getting good grades for college.

After school, I gazed at Tyrone's old bed, wondering how he was doing in college. He called, as if he knew I was thinking about him, and I picked up.

"Hey, what's up? How's it going?" I asked.

"It's alright. Really messed up my shoulder. I can hardly move it. I'm going to physical therapy, but the doctor said I can't play football anymore."

He sounded tired; his voice cracked as he spoke. I held onto the phone, unsure what to say, wishing he was better. Football was a part of who he was in high school. It's how I knew him. I didn't know who he was going to be now.

…

I knew Mom would freak out if I tried to have a party after what we went through with Tyrone. But I occasionally had a few friends over to hang out when she and Norman weren't there.

One Saturday afternoon, Keith came over with Jamie, Coop, and Hakim to drink while my mom was out at an all-day event with Aunt Jeanette and Norman. Hakim had a thirty pack of Natural Light beers sitting on the front steps of the house, with his hat turned backwards on his head, while the sun beamed on him seemingly without a care in the world. Jamie, Coop, and I were in the basement making drinks from Norman's bar and putting water back in the whiskey bottle to make it look like nothing was gone. We played pool while Keith was putting music on in the living room. We all laughed and talked about the plans for a party for the night.

"I'll go take a shower and get dressed then we'll head to the party," I said already feeling buzzed.

While I was in the shower, I heard the front door slam and my mom say, "What's going on in here?"

I came out, ran downstairs in my towel, and acted confused.

"Are you guys drinking?" My mom asked.

"I didn't know they were drinking. I was in the shower." I said.

Aunt Jeanette and my mom shook their heads. "Your friends have to go," my mom said. Keith and the rest of the guys gathered their things, gave Hakim and I a nod and left with their heads hanging low as if our moms were scolding them too.

After my friends left, my mom and aunt spoke to us.

"Y'all really think you're White. Hakim out here drinking in the open. You can't do what your White friends do." My mom and aunt said together.

They didn't yell. They continuously shook their heads in utter disappointment. I didn't say anything. I thought it wasn't such a big deal, we weren't having a huge party like my brother. I also thought, *We're not trying to be White*. But when I looked at my mom and aunt's face, I knew we let them down. I couldn't see my friends for weeks for punishment; it seemed like years.

Later, Keith got his license and a brand-new black Chevy Blazer that became our official ride and new life of freedom to get around town, get beer, and go to parties while listening to Keith's CD collection. When we went down to Newark, Hakim and I looked the oldest, so we were able to go in and buy beer. Then Keith drove us back and we drank the beers at his house. We heard about a party at Hakim's friend's house, drove over in Keith's car and tried to hook up with the younger girls there. Sometimes we went to parties with seniors who were about to graduate. A couple of them were Black kids with White friends like me and Hakim, giving us a sense of what was to come when we were all about to graduate. The look in their eyes seemed like they knew those were their final times together.

A big event for us was when we all went to the Dave Matthews Band concert at Garden State Art Center. Hot 97.1's Summer Jam would've played hip hop, rap, and R&B, but I wanted to check out this concert of a band I'd grown to like over the years and to hang out with my friends. We sat in Keith's car along with other friends in the parking lot all day where we drank beers in the sun, smoked weed, and talked to other kids from all over New Jersey while the band played.

The concert and a lot of my hanging out with Keith and our friends cost money that I was starving for. The money from working during the summer was gone, and my odd jobs of moving furniture and mowing lawns here and there wasn't enough.

I would ask my mom and Norman for money.

"Ma, can I have twenty dollars?"

She'd give it to me out of her purse.

A few days later, "Ma, can I have ten dollars?"

She'd hand it to me letting out a sigh.

One day, I came in to ask for money, "Ma, can I have . . ."

Mom interrupted me, "Tony, you need to get a job. I can't keep giving you money. I'm not like your friends' parents. Norman and I have been talking. He knows the manager of the Marco Polo Italian restaurant. He got you a job there as a busboy."

"What? I don't want to work there. Everyone goes there. They'll see me. Keith doesn't need to work," I said.

"Well, we're not giving you any more money. Norman will take you over there on Sunday. We'll get you some clothes to wear."

I stormed off to my room.

Sunday came and Norman drove me over to the Italian restaurant. I looked around the dimly lit room with round tables and white tablecloths. There weren't a lot of people there, I guess because of the time we came in. Norman introduced me to the manager, and we shook hands. I kept my head down and peeked at faces to see if I recognized anyone.

The manager showed me what I'd be doing: picking up dishes from the tables, bringing them to the back, cleaning them, and helping clean up later. I watched as the waiters took orders from customers and wished I was at least one of them. A busboy was the lowest on the totem pole. I looked at Norman with fire in my eyes, and in that moment, I hated him.

I cleaned a few dishes as I looked out to the front from the back, looking at the customers. I prayed none of them were Keith, his family, or anyone else who knew me.

That's how it went for weeks. I did my homework then dressed in my black pants, black shoes, and white shirt then walked over to the restaurant where I went right to the back and hid the rest of the night. I speedily got dishes off the tables, sprayed them clean, ate cheesy manicotti and baked ziti while watching the customers in the front. No one I knew ever came.

After about a month, I told Keith I was working at the restaurant. He said, "Wow, that's awesome man." He told me he had a job during the summer. It was something his dad thought was important and something for him to do while some other kids went to their summer homes. I later pulled out the cash I made from under the mattress and said that was my last day. I thought of the job. I was tired of it, and I had learned the lesson. It wasn't only about the money; it was about doing what I had to do, even though I didn't want to do it.

...

One night in the fall, I walked home all the way from Keith's house. I was on my street, a few houses away from my home. Only a few of the streetlights were on that could capture my body wearing a hoodie in the light. Exhausted, I was feeling relieved to see my house coming up, thinking of finally falling onto my bed to pass out. A car pulled up in the darkness and blinded me with its light.

"Where are you going? Let me see some ID," a voice said.

I partly noticed the police car with the lights on top. "I live right there," I said pointing at my house.

"Yeah? Where's your ID?" The cop repeated.

"I don't have an ID. I live right there," I said pointing, growing annoyed, and worried. *Why wouldn't they just let me go?*

"Where are you coming from?" he said.

"Huh? My friend's house," I said, letting out a sigh of exasperation.

"OK. We'll let you go," he said.

I turned and walked as the car drove slowly next to me. When I got to my door and opened it, the car pulled away. *Fuck them.*

I went up to my room and paced before sitting on the edge of my bed to calm down. *Why'd they treat me like that?* Shame and frustration rumbled inside of me. I'd went through these years trying to get people to treat me like a human, not to make me feel like something else.

I felt silly recalling the time I rode in Keith's car. "Hey, see that guy over there on the bench, near the train station. Can you describe him without using his skin color?" I asked, grinning to make us comfortable.

Keith paused and smiled, "Dude, what? What do you mean?" He smirked. "Uh, that's a guy with dreadlocks." We laughed and drove on as if I had tricked and defeated racism.

I slowly remembered riding down the highway with my cousins. I was sitting in the back of the hunchback car with my hood up over my head when bright lights pulled up behind us and the siren went off. The police walked up to my cousin and asked if we had any weapons.

He smirked at me and said, "Yeah, get out your sharp school pencils."

They told us to get out the car. My cousin sucked his teeth and shook his head. I wanted to run away. I snapped out of it and went to my mom's room.

Sound from the TV came through the door, so I lightly knocked to see if they were awake.

My mom said, "Come in."

She was getting adjusted on her side of the bed while Norman slept.

"Hey, are you okay?" she asked. I didn't normally come in her room like this and not this late at night.

I sat down on a chair next to her bed. I tried to tell her the story.

"I was walking home, and some cops just flashed their lights in my face. Right outside the house. I kept trying to tell them I lived here. But they didn't want to hear me. They didn't want to believe me. I kept trying to tell them." I was speaking fast, my heart racing, and it was all rushing to my face, pushing tears into my eyes. "Why'd they treat me like that?"

My mom sat up and put her glasses on with a look of concern. She let out a sigh.

"I'm sorry. I'm sorry this happened to you. Some people including cops can act that way because of the way you look. But everything will be okay," she said, consoling me. Her last words hung in the night. *Everything will be okay.* My worry, pain, and anger seemed to melt away . . .

. . .

Family would sometimes come over to our house for barbecues and hang out to watch movies or play cards. It was like having the family together when we were little. Norm would be on the grill while we listened to music and laughed with aunts, uncles, and cousins in the backyard, or watched movies in the living room, and played pool in the basement. I always loved being with family; they were a piece of me, my history, and they would always love who I was no matter what changes I went through.

We'd still occasionally go to Grandma's on the weekends. But the times there were changing. On the way to Grandma's house, Mom told me about Uncle Clift. Over the last few months, he would go missing from Grandma's for days. She said he was in the basement, and no one would see him, and that he was doing drugs. I almost couldn't believe the drugs part. *No, not him.* When we got there, I walked into the kitchen where I used to dance while eating my breakfast and Uncle Clift would come up through the basement door and smack me upside the head to tell me to "Stop dancing and eat." Now, I gazed at the basement door and wondered if he was down there.

We sat at the dining room table, the same table where my uncle stood over me as a child, his hand wrapped around mine, guiding my pencil while drawing a poster for an art contest. The fridge in the kitchen still had a newspaper article of me with the winning ribbon. We'd spent many family gatherings at this dining room table. We said prayers for Thanksgiving and Christmas dinners of succulent turkeys, hams, and creamy mac and cheese. I never forgot, even as I sat there. I wondered if my dear uncle would come upstairs to see us like those old times.

I imagined him down there in the darkness with grimy walls that crowded him where hope died. He'd sit on that ragged couch near the pool table leaning over the coffee table with needles and vials strewn where he used to draw me dragons with sharp teeth and jagged wings, spitting fire. I'd watch the muscles in his hand work the pencil and be astonished by the life he created on the paper. He was special and had a gift.

I greeted Grandma with a kiss on the cheek as she sat in her favorite chair near the window and phone.

Then we sat down at the dining room table. Grandma and Mom talked more as I looked around the room. There were pictures of me, my brothers, and cousins as kids, black and white pictures of my mom in lacy dresses with Aunt Esther and Aunt Yvonne when they lived in the South before Pop brought them up to live in Summit. In front of me was a drawing Uncle Clift did of Grandma with rosy cheeks, a wide smile, and in her custom pink church hat with lace that she'd wear to go to the church next door. When it was time to go, I passed the basement door, placing my hand over it. *Bye, Uncle Clift.*

Weeks went by and no one knew where Uncle Clift was staying. I heard stories of him staying in the terrible parts of Newark where people high on drugs roamed around the streets lifelessly, unknown to the world, and not knowing the time or the sun on them. I cried at times thinking about where my uncle was. I was told he called a few relatives for money or stopped by for some food. My mom also told me he had contracted multiple diseases, including the most saddening, AIDS.

The disease was new to us, and it was new to the world. We didn't know how to treat him or care for him. But we loved him and couldn't continue to turn our backs.

One day, Mom was on the phone in the kitchen.

"Where are you? Up the street on River Road? Yeah, you can come over." She hung up the phone and let out a sigh.

I came downstairs. Mom told me, "Tony, your Uncle Clift is coming over. Bring me some wash rags and a towel so he can wash up."

I could tell she was sad after that sigh and by the look in her eyes. I ran up and down the stairs and handed her the wash rags, towel, and soap.

The doorbell rang. I sat upstairs peeking through the railing to the front door when it opened. All I could see was the top of his body. But, just from that, I could tell he was a fraction of his former self. What was once a full head of slick black hair was now thin and balding; his strong chin and smile were now taken over by dark patches on his cheeks, and he was gaunt. I couldn't move.

I don't know why I didn't go downstairs to say hi to my dear uncle. Maybe I was afraid of the diseases. Maybe I was afraid to see him that way. It almost felt like he wasn't the same uncle I grew up with. I was caught in the moment. It was like I was watching death for the first time; he was ghostly, as if he hardly existed. I was amazed, horrified, and yet I still loved my uncle.

I gripped the rails, sweating, as my mother moved gingerly around him, perhaps unsure of how to touch him. She gave him the wash rags and towels and he went into the bathroom downstairs near the foyer. My mom went to the kitchen. I sat upstairs and continued to watch.

About fifteen minutes later, he came out and my mom met him outside the bathroom with a plastic bag of food: slices of pound cake, chips, a sandwich, and a can of soda. She finally gave him a hug as she opened the door and watched him walk away.

I came running down the stairs to console my mother who was weeping in the doorway.

...

A couple weeks later, Uncle Clift was in the hospital. My mom and other cousins visited him, but I wouldn't go. Mom told me about the tubes in his body, how frail he was, and how he was losing his eyesight. I couldn't bear to see him that way.

We had a family get together at our house. Most of the kids, including me, were in the TV room, squeezed in on the wraparound couch, floor, and extra chairs. Mom and some others were in other places cooking food, eating, or playing cards. We were all together this time, which sounds easy to say but not easy to do. We usually had a party where at least someone didn't make it. We were all here for once, for something that turned out to be more than a party.

We were watching a movie that had a character who was a drug addict. His father was a preacher and saw his son filled with "the evils of drugs." He prayed for his son before he went into another room, got his gun, looked at his son, and <u>he pulled the trigger.</u>[10]

At that moment, the phone rang. It was a call from the hospital; they said our uncle Clift had just passed away. The house was silent, then it erupted into a cacophony of grief. These sounds of agony were unknown to me. Our family had never experienced losing someone like this, someone so close to us.

I walked in a daze as it happened around me. Mom hugged Aunt Esther and others in the kitchen. It was excruciatingly painful to see my mother cry with her red cheeks and trembling lips. A few of my cousins went to the dining room and some to the living room, sat on the green leather couches, sniffling as one of them put a hand on the other's shoulder. I stood in the hallway amidst the house of mayhem. Tyrone was still at college, unable to share the grief with me or help me understand

---

10

a loss. Aunt Jeanette hugged me and wiped the tears from my cheeks. "He's in a better place," she said.

Soon after was the funeral. I didn't go, or I don't remember standing over his closed casket as it was lowered into the earth. I wasn't ready for it. It was the first time I'd dealt with death. I think I was devoid of much feeling; I didn't know how to feel or express myself. He was a big part of the beginning of my life, and I didn't realize how much more of my life I'd have without him. I'd walk around my house, go to school, and continue hanging out with my friends, almost as if nothing happened.

From time to time, I'd go to Grandma's and look at the picture Uncle Clift drew of her with the laced church hat and a golden-like smile that lit up the room. We found other drawings throughout the house, in the drawers and cabinets in the dining room, like the one he drew of the family from my childhood, a caricature that we all loved: Grandma cooking in the kitchen with smoke pluming while she was talking on the phone, Aunt Esther dragging Devin by the hand as he cried,

Cory choking Tyrone for stealing his bike again, my mom falling down at our old apartment, and finally me on my scooter, grinning.

The images still filled us with memories of those times and of him. When we went in the basement, I looked at the indentation on the couch where he used to sleep. It was so dark, the room filled with blackness even with the sun outside. I imagined him there for a moment and shook my head in disbelief. *He shouldn't be gone.*

When we got home, I went to my room and unfolded the picture of a dragon he drew for me as kid. My eyes following the penciled lines, admiring the sharp teeth and deadly eyes. It all made me miss him more. It was unfair; his life was over, and his talent was taken away.

One Saturday afternoon, Keith, Hakim, Jamie, and Coop came over to my house to hang out and do some drinking. We were in the basement sitting at the high-top table taking a break from playing pool and drinking some of Norman's whiskey from the bar. We were talking about what we were going to do that night, what parties were going on, and girls.

There was a pause in our conversation, and I immediately felt like I needed to talk to them. I told them how Uncle Clift recently passed away. Their eyes trembled as one of them placed a hand on my shoulder. Then tears fell from Hakim's eyes as he told us he saw Uncle Clift in the darkness of that basement, holding onto the drugs that lost him. My chest ached. I'd never heard this from him, and it hurt to see my cousin, someone so large and strong, break from pain in his heart. With a shaking voice, Keith then told us he still thinks about his brother that passed away from drugs. We couldn't stop the tears.

We all seemed to be at the start of our lives, trying to understand death and loss. There was confliction in their eyes. Was it pain, anger or grief as their faces dropped and eye lids filled? Some of us walked off, went to separate areas of the house, some to the living room and sat on the leather couches, and some outside on the front steps with the sun and fresh air. It was all new to me: the hurt on Hakim's face and the image of my uncle in the basement with the drugs in his hands. The sadness in Keith's eyes brought empathy for a friend I didn't know I had. I didn't think I'd feel sorrow for him. His family seemed to have a better life, impervious to heartache. I found it wasn't all sunshine in the hills of Summit—dark clouds rained on the top of hills as well. I knew we all grieved and cared about each other. And I didn't want anyone else in my family to <u>die</u>.[11]

11

Growing Up

As junior year was ending, I'd come home from the final days of school with books from my locker. I thought of senior year coming up: I needed to prepare to take the SAT tests in the fall and work on college applications, but I really wanted to go to Keith's and hang out.

I heard my mom talking to Tyrone on the phone about losing the college money he received for playing football and how she had to pay a lot more. I watched her and went out with Keith, not knowing how this would affect my life.

For months, my mom wasn't her jovial self. The patio furniture company, Wellington, closed so she needed another job. It weighed on her at the dining room table while she looked at bills as she was spending her severance pay to keep us in Summit. Her shoulders were raised so tight. She got her real estate license and seemed happy to have the business cards, but she didn't sell enough homes. It was just something to do until she found something more secure.

One day in August, my mom called me into the dining room.

"Hey Tony, can you come in here?" she asked.

"Yeah, Ma," I responded, walking in, and grabbing a seat next to her at the table.

"I know that you enjoy living in Summit, being here with your friends and your family. But … I decided to take a new job in Florida. I tried to find another way, but the jobs up here pay too much. I need to get a lower paying job so Tyrone can get financial aid." She took a deep breath. "So, me and Norman are going to move down there at the end of the summer. They're only giving us thirty days." She sighed.

I thought about my friends and the path I was on. *I only have one more year in high school …*

"No. I'm not going. I don't want to go," I said sternly, looking my mother in the eyes.

"You know, they have good schools in Florida too. You could go down there," she said, consoling me.

"No," I said.

She spoke as my mind wandered, lost in memories and the time ahead of me: prom, final parties, girls, and preparing for college. I had a path, and I wasn't going to change it.

"I'm not going."

She looked back at me, her eyes shook with an almost sense of pride and fear of losing her baby.

She knew how I felt. Her mom moved her and her siblings up to New Jersey from the south when she was a child, and her grades got worse. She knew I was close to going to college, something she never got to do.

"Okay. Okay. I understand. I've trusted you in the decisions you've made so far," she said.

The last of the summer days were rushed with final family barbecues at our house, packing, and hanging out with friends till the day everything had to change. My mind was a whirlwind; I had to find somewhere to live. Mom called family, asking if they could let me stay with them my final year.

Aunt Yvonne was quick to say, "I'd love to, Evelyn." I'd imagine my aunt saying yes while holding her Bible in her hand and praying to the Lord for me and my family.

Mom flipped through brochures of apartments her new company sent her to help find a place. She chose one of the first places she saw: a new apartment in a new apartment building in a new gated community that had a pool, tennis courts, and a gym. It was within her budget. She was amazed at the images, though thoughts of my wellbeing lingered.

Tyrone was packing up his room, putting more clothes into his trunk to spend more time at school during holidays and breaks. Cory put any furniture and clothes that he could into his and his girlfriend's car. Norman got the Dynasty ready for their long drive to Florida.

I stood in the street next to the moving truck as the movers packed up the last box of things for my parents. Looking up through the green tree limbs to the sun above, I took in the moment.

My bags sat at the curb as Aunt Yvonne pulled up to take me to her place to live. Cory put his final bag in the back of his Trans Am, almost ready to pull off to move in with his girlfriend. And Tyrone put a small box in the trunk of his friend's car before they headed off to a college dorm room. We all came together one last time for hugs and looked at the house one more time. For a moment, I flashed back to those times of when we moved in, the parties my brother had, playing pool in the basement, the time my parents caught us drinking, the time with my uncle Clift and the time of his demise, and the times we all lived together.

This is it. This is where it all ends, and we all go our separate ways to be on our own. I think I'm ready.

...

I moved my trunk upstairs into the extra bedroom across the hall from my cousin Steven's room. I sat on the bed, exhaled, and prepared for my new life. I was unfamiliar with the room and its surroundings: there was a single bed, a dresser, a closet with someone else's clothes, and pictures of my aunt's family around. My cousin's room was across the hall next to the bathroom, and my aunt and uncle's room was next to mine. I felt lost and alone for a minute. I got up quickly to hang out with my cousin and aunt hoping that I'd feel better.

Aunt Yvonne sat in the kitchen. I gave her a wide hug, wrapping my arms around her voluminous body filled with kindness and a love of God. As I embraced her, I held on tightly, appreciating her for helping me.

I got a few calls from friends offering for me to live with them. One of the first people to call me was Keith.

"Hey man, I spoke to my parents. You wanna stay over our house? We feel so bad with your parents leaving and you not really having any place to live. I know you're staying with your aunt. But you can stay at our place sometimes too."

I held the phone in my hand and looked at Aunt Yvonne. "I'm okay, man. Maybe some other time. I'm with family now."

It was the fall of senior year, and I needed to apply to college. On a Saturday morning, I walked into a classroom with other kids from nearby towns to take the SAT. The questions from my SAT preparation book still swirled in my head. I nervously sat down, knowing I needed to get a high score on this test to get into college. A person at the front of the room told us to start as the time began to click and we hurriedly put our pens to paper. After a few moments, I stared at my answers, wondering if I selected the right choices, then looked around the room and noticed the other kids constantly writing and circling without hesitation. *I need to focus.* I leaned in and sped through the remaining questions with determination. I let out a deep breath of relief as I gave it all the energy I had.

I tried to forget the test by spending time with friends and partying. I was at a house party with Keith, Coop, and a bunch of other kids, drinking alcohol, playing beer pong in the kitchen, and blasting music. The cops came through the front door, and everyone scattered out the back door. I was Spiderman as I jumped off the balcony and ran through the trees as fast as I could, like it was a game to dodge the flashlights of the police. I even pushed my friend, Ann, into a police officer for me to get away. *Eh, she'll be okay.* I ran behind houses and hid in bushes as the police cars drove away from the house. I got away.

I needed some money. Mom sent Aunt Yvonne some money for groceries for me, but I needed more to hang out. I went into the career office at school, like I used to do, and asked for any odd jobs. They gave me a landscaping job for one house near town. I figured nothing could be worse than that busboy job I had. When I got home to Aunt Yvonne's, I immediately called the guy and told him I'll come mow his lawn. I hung up the phone and realized I had no way to get to the job and do it. I took a deep breath and went upstairs to ask my uncle Sam. After I explained I needed to borrow his truck, a lawnmower and other equipment, he just said "Yeah, alright."

I got to the job with Uncle Sam's truck and equipment. While mowing the lawn, a neighbor across the street came over and asked me if I could mow their lawn. "Sure" I said. As I was mowing that neighbor's lawn, another neighbor came over to me and asked me to mow their lawn when I mow the others once a week. "Yes!" I leapt for joy inside; I was now making almost a couple hundred dollars a week for myself.

A couple weeks later, I was back at my aunt's dining room table, sitting for hours and days hunched over stacks of applications, mulling over the results from those tests. I looked at my score: 1050 out of 1600. I did well on the math portion but not so well on the reading portion. It was lower than Keith's score by more than a hundred points. I considered taking the tests again.

For now, I flipped through brochures from prospective colleges thinking about which one would give me the best future. The brochure from American University excited me. I checked it's ranking in the book of U.S. colleges, and it was in the top fifty out of hundreds of schools. I imagined being in Washington D.C. and vising the White House. I put brochures from Villanova, Lehigh, Loyola, and others close by as options because I'd heard their names before on TV and from other friends. There were no brochures from historically Black universities. I didn't expect any; the universities on *The Cosby Show* and in movies weren't real to me. They weren't on the list of top universities as I flipped through the book. None of my friends or family mentioned them. The decision was mine based on all I knew and wanted.

I tried to fill out the applications and financial aid documents as best I could. I always knew I was going to college, yet unsure how I'd pay for it, as if it would magically happen. I looked at the financial aid papers as part of the path to my goal. I needed it. For a moment, I wasn't sure if all the information was correct. I didn't know how important it was to make sure.

The part of my application that I was the proudest of was my essay. To me, it was the best thing I'd ever written and created. The same feelings of when I was a child writing my first poem came back. I read it over and over; the words described how I decided to stay in

Summit without my family, and how I was ready to make this life for myself and go on to college.

But my head was pounding, the papers became blurry, and my motivation was fading as I sank into the chair. My parents hadn't gone to college, neither had Cory, and although Tyrone was able to help a little from his experience, he wasn't here. I was by myself as the papers seemed to bury me. My eyes swelled and watered. The phone rang.

Aunt Yvonne picked it up in the kitchen. "Hello. Hey, Evelyn. Yeah, Tony's here. You want to talk to him? OK, here you go." She held the phone away from her face for a moment. "Tony, your mother is on the phone."

I got up and got the phone from my aunt, stretching the phone cord to the living room.

"Hello," I said.

"Heyyy. How are you doing, Son? How's everything going?" she asked.

I paused, quiet for a moment. "Okay," I said, while walking to another room.

"What's wrong?" she probed.

Tears rolled down my cheek and onto the phone. "Ma, I don't know what I'm doing." I said.

"I'm sorry. I'm so sorry I can't be there," she said, also crying over the phone. "You'll be alright though. Everything will be alright. Okay?"

I became more upset hearing her sniffles. My stomach felt sick for her pain. I couldn't bear to hear my mother hurt as I stood in the living room. I tried to stay hopeful for both of us. "Okay, I'm sorry Ma. It'll be okay." I wiped the tears and immediately started to feel better. I hung up the phone and finished the paperwork.

...

A couple of weeks later, I was in class laughing with Keith when the teacher told me to go see my guidance counselor after class. *Must be about college.* I walked to my guidance counselor's office without worry.

I knocked on the glass of her door, and she motioned me to come in. She was shorter than me with brown hair, and she looked at me worriedly. My smile quickly faded.

"Tony, I've noticed your address has changed. Where are you living?"

I swallowed, "I'm living at my aunt's house."

"Unfortunately, Tony, your aunt is not your guardian. You need to be living with your parents or a guardian in Summit to go to school here."

I started to sweat, "What do you mean?" I inquired.

"You don't live with your parents. Or someone who is lawfully your guardian. I'm sorry, you may not be able to go to school here."

"But I've been going to school here," I said.

"In order for you to keep going here, you have to emancipate yourself," she said.

"What does that mean?" I asked. My heart was racing.

"You'll have to be independent of your parents in order for you to keep going here."

"What? That's like saying I don't have parents, like I don't have a mom," I said, aching at the thought of being without my mom.

"I'm sorry, Tony. This is what you have to do," she said, handing me the paperwork to sign.

I signed them and left the office; I'd left my family, and I was definitely by myself now.

...

Shortly after, I was out to dinner with a friend and his mom at a restaurant in town. It was a casual place that everyone always looked forward to going to with TVs, a bar, and people laughing, including us. I don't recall exactly what we were talking about, but I remember his blonde-haired mom with glasses spoke to me with her southern twang. My tall friend sat next to her with his glasses on, smiling as well. Both of us laughed again at the times we had to get to this point—hanging out at his house listening to James Brown, catching the sun rise, going to his private country club to swim and eat, watching his swim meets, and partying in his basement. His mom said it was great that I was planning to go to college, and she smiled.

I smiled back and … I blacked out.

When I opened my eyes, I was in the hospital. The lights were bright; I squinted to see. White sheets lay over me, and a tube was connected from my arm to something else. My chest was connected to a heart monitor that beeped. My eyes blinked. *What happened?* My chest started to pound.

A doctor wearing a white coat came in with a clipboard. She checked the monitor. I was dizzy but focused enough to ask her. "What happened?"

"It seems you had some sort of anxiety attack or palpitations. We're still running some tests. But you seem to be okay. You must've passed out. Your friends ensured you got here."

"What?" I tried to remember what happened back at the restaurant. But the last image I recalled was laughing with my friend and his mom.

"It's okay. You're okay. Just relax. We'll be back to check on you." The doctor left. I watched her leave and looked around: the TV on the wall, my legs under the sheet, and the darkness outside the window.

I was all alone. Tears formed in my eyes, and I grabbed my chest. *What am I going to do?* I closed my eyes, took a few deep breaths, and tried to relax.

The doctor came back in and said I could go home. "If this happens again, just take a few deep breaths, in and out, slowly. It will be okay."

"Okay," I said. I just wanted to feel okay and never have this happen again. But I practiced the deep breaths and felt a release. *I'll be okay.*

...

Weeks later, a bunch of us went down the shore for the weekend to a friend's parents' house to hang out. Keith and I pulled up in his Chevy Blazer while Hakim and a few others got out of other cars and walked into the house. As I neared, I saw the house was multiple levels with large windows facing the backyard; it also had a dock and pier. More people pulled their cars into the driveway and came into the house with food, bags of clothes, cases of beer, and bottles of alcohol. There were no parents around as I watched the kids coming and going from the house. I grabbed a beer and a seat. I was waiting for the girls, one in particular.

We hung out outside for hours into the night, drinking, and talking near the dock. Lisa and her friends walked over to us. Coop was dating one of her friends with short brown hair; she was taller and smarter than Coop and smiled while making fun of him. He'd take it because she was his girl. Keith liked one of her other friends with blonde hair and big boobs. She was also able to match Keith's smart-ass comments, though he didn't say much to her, probably due to his attraction to her boobs. All these girls were younger than us, yet they had our interest.

I grinned while remembering Lisa's straight blonde hair that I used to run my fingers through during the months we were together. She maintained a small smile with her tiny mouth that I used to cover with mine at her friends' parties where we were introduced and saw each other every week. I stood up and said hi as we gave each other a cordial hug then made jokes at each other to further show we were friends, since our phone calls gradually stopped months ago. It was how some of my teenage relationships tended to end—without much communication from me to end it—like a balloon intentionally let go in the wind for it to fly away.

Now our eyes met and darted away, and I gazed at her mouth and slender body, feeling myself pulled towards her as if she was always mine and I was always hers. I snapped out of it remembering how she moved on to someone else, an artsy guy with long blond hair.

I went back to partying with Keith, Hakim, and some others as I watched Lisa out of the corner of my eye. After a few more drinks, Lisa and I looked at each other and went inside the house together.

In the house, people were loud, laughing, music was blasting, the kitchen was a mess of food on the counters and table, and the house smelled of weed and cigarettes. We went upstairs and looked for an empty room. We found one and sat on the edge of the bed.

"Hey," we said, giggling.

"I've missed you," I said, smiling.

"Aw, me too," she said, beaming.

We leaned in and kissed. I pulled away. "But what about Oscar?"

"Oh, we're not together right now," she said.

We kissed more. "Remember what we always promised each other? Even if we weren't together, we were going to be each other's first to lose our virginity with. Are we going to do it?" I said, pulling out my wallet with the circle ring impression from the condom showing from the outside.

"Oh, yeah, I remember. I wanted to tell you. I already did it with Oscar," she said, still gleaming.

I moved away, slumped in disappointment. "But you said you'll be my first. I wanted it to be with you."

"I'm sorry, I know. But I was with him, and it just kind of happened. Really, it's no big deal. It's okay, we can still do it." The final words felt like pity for me; I couldn't take it.

"No, it's okay. It's not right, now." I put my wallet away and went back to the party. *I'll find someone else.*

...

At school, I sat with friends in the back of my Advanced Math class and raised my hand with the right answer time after time. I was getting perfect scores and grades on my tests. I liked how much the teacher treasured me, calling on me to come up to the board and praising me in front of the class. I gloated at my high scores, feeling proud. But the enjoyment was momentary; I walked out of the classroom without much thought for mathematics, no fire in my belly to continue calculating calculus.

Later, I laughed with my friend Ann in Advanced Spanish. She made fun of me when I messed up my grammar while reenacting scenes from the movie *Scream* in Spanish for the class assignment. Her red hair swayed as she turned and chuckled when I said something like, "No esta hablamos espanol usted."

I went to Economics class, sat in the back with a few friends and strained through the lesson. I was joking around, not caring much about what the teacher was saying. In my head, I knew this class was a good path for college to study business or finance to make some good money. I sat in class and imagined working on Wall Street or something, one of those guys in a suit walking past the New York Stock Exchange with a briefcase, and then having one of these houses in Summit to come home to.

I spent the end of class listening to a girl named Amy complain about her boyfriend. "He doesn't call me.

We don't do anything." I remembered Ann saying I should date girls my own age.

I leaned in and said, "If you were with me, you wouldn't have that problem." I shocked myself, like I was some pimp or Casanova with the girls. She flung her long brown hair around, looked at me, and smiled with full lips. She gave me her number.

At night, I worked on my homework at the dining room table. After, I spoke to Amy on the phone for hours in the living room. My confidence was still sky high after what I said to her in class, like I knew she would want to talk to me. The conversation went something like this:

"Hi Mrs. Johnson. Is Amy there? This is Tony," I said to her mom politely as she picked up the house phone.

"Hi, Tony. Yes, let me get her," she said. I heard ruffling like she covered the phone as she yelled, "Amy, phone!"

I laid on my aunt's couch and wrapped the cord of the phone around my finger as I waited.

"Hi," Amy coyly answered. I felt her smile on the other end of the phone.

We talked about nothing and everything, jumping from one topic to another:

What was she doing, and did she finish the Economics homework? She did the homework, which I wasn't surprised because she always had answers in class. I asked what her friends were doing this weekend, and she said nothing much, but her close friend Samara was going to have a party for her boyfriend soon that we could go to. She told me she came back from gymnastics practice, but she couldn't do much since she hurt her leg. For a moment, I felt bad for her; I wanted her to do what she'd wanted to do, like my brother when he hurt his shoulder. I asked her about her parents; her mom seemed nice on the phone. She got quiet and said she doesn't really talk to her biological dad. I got quiet too; I understood and immediately felt what she felt—disappointment.

I remembered she said her previous boyfriend never wanted to do anything. So, I asked, "Would you like to go to the movies sometime?" She said yes.

We sat in class and gave each other looks like we were waiting for the class to end to be next to each other in the halls. We continued to talk on the phone as I waited for us to see each other. She came to pick me up in her green Honda Accord and took us to the movies. It was like my first real date; I paid for tickets and popcorn, and we held hands. I never did much with my previous girlfriends. We just hooked up at parties or talked on the phone. Going on a date to the movies was like something I'd only seen in the movies.

When I wasn't at Keith's, I drove Uncle Sam's pickup truck to Amy's house. As I turned down her street, I realized her house was around the corner from my old house on Iris Road. I always thought of the times living at my home when I visited her.

I slammed the truck's rusted door and dusted off my pants from the dingy seats. My uncle's orange garbage cans from his job were still in the back as the moonlight shined on the truck's dents. My heart warmed as I felt its cold door handle, feeling proud it was my uncle's truck. Moments ago, he grunted, "Okay," when I asked if I could borrow the truck. It was the same "okay" he gave me to drive the truck to go mow people's lawns using his lawnmowers and those garbage pails for grass clippings. Or I'd drive to parties, up the hills to Keith's, among million-dollar homes and alongside other shiny cars. Sometimes I brought Amy in this truck with me. Tonight, we were at her house.

I walked to the house, carrying my backpack with my bottle of alcohol inside that I bought in Newark with my fake ID. Amy let me in, and I said hi to her mom in the kitchen. Her stepdad was somewhere else in the house. We headed down to her basement to watch a movie like usual. We talked about going to college, and she said she wanted to go to school for Marine Biology. I immediately thought, *She knows what she wants to be. I don't know what I want to do.*

We watched *Schindler's List*, then I put on the Dave Matthews Band's song "Crash"[12] and we danced slowly. We sat on the couch and the music played on while my hands moved all over Amy's body, our mouths intertwined. Our clothes remained on. I let other girls touch me in more places, but I removed Amy's hands when she grabbed near my crotch. I didn't want it to be over too soon, but I knew I wanted to lose my virginity with her. Just not right now.

A few days later, I went to lacrosse practice. We had a big game coming up against a rival, Delbarton. But I had to talk to Coach about something important to me.

As we ended our huddle and everyone started going home, I took a gulp and walked over to Coach.

"Hey Coach, I'm not going to be able to make it to the game. I have to go visit a college."

"Ok, Tony. Well, I'm disappointed. This is a big game. We're going to have to give your position to someone else. You may be moved down to a lower line

12

126

for a while," he said looking down at me. He could eat me with his bear size.

"I'm sorry, I have to go. College is important to me," I said, walking away.

That weekend, Aunt Esther drove me up to Villanova. In the car, I imagined my friend Coop playing in my position at the lacrosse game, swinging the lacrosse stick as he ran down the field with my other teammates and scoring. I smiled because it was Coop.

My eyes widened as we arrived at Villanova's campus. I was amazed by the massive gray buildings and students walking around. *This could be me.*

We walked to the front of the main building to meet two people. One was a girl I used to be fond of named Autumn who went to Summit High school but was a year older than me. Tyrone tried to hook me up with her since he knew her older brother, but it didn't work out. Now, she was going to Villanova. She still looked great with her long brown hair, full lips, and curvy body. The other was a kid that went to Newark Academy and also got accepted to Villanova. I immediately thought, *See, I made the right decision not to go to Newark Academy. I made it to a great university just like him.*

She told me the place was great; she loved her first year there, and the dorms and people were cool. We spoke about the laptop buying program the university had for the new students, which I was keenly interested in, since I needed help buying a computer. But I was also more interested in how she spoke about the men's basketball team. I already knew the school had a great team, and I couldn't wait to see a game. On the way home, I thought about what I just saw at Villanova and how I could walk around the campus. But I didn't know how I'd pay for it all.

At one of the next lacrosse practices, I noticed I wasn't playing as much as I used to. I watched other players play more and prepare for another game coming up. I lowered my head in discontent. But I had to have another discussion with my coach about visiting universities.

"Coach, can I talk to you?" I asked, expecting him to growl with anger.

"What's up?" he asked.

"I want to visit Lehigh." I said, waiting for backlash.

"They have a great lacrosse program there. I can speak to the coach about you getting on the team."

I thought about it for a moment. "That's okay. I'm going to college for an education. I don't plan to play sports. I need to focus."

...

On the weekend, I packed up my bags and Keith picked me up to bring me to his house, fulfilling his offer to let me stay with him and his family.

When I got there, I said hi to Keith's Mom and thanked her. I grabbed some Kudos snack bars that she only bought for me because Keith told her I'm the only one that eats them. I didn't have the chocolate-covered granola bars at home, so they were always a treat at his house. Keith's ugly pug dog rubbed snot on my pants as I pet him before going upstairs. Keith led me past a couple of guest rooms down the hall to my room.

When I opened the door, the room was filled with warmth and love; pictures of Keith's brother he lost were on the walls. The bed was made with plaid bedding and fluffy pillows. Keith showed me the door to the bathroom and opened another attached door that led to his room. I dropped my bags, and we went downstairs for dinner.

When we came into the kitchen, Keith's dad was finishing making dinner while Keith's mom set the table. I sat next to Keith with a view of the outside deck and pool below, treetops, and other homes in the distance.

I observed Keith's dad on the grill outside, flipping steaks and salmon overlooking the pool next to the patio table and patio umbrella I sold him from my mom's old job. He brought the food into the house, filling our plates. I thought about how I'd like to make food for my family in a home like this one day.

"What are you guys doing tonight? You guys be safe."

"Nothing much, a couple of people are going to come over," Keith said.

"We're proud of both of you. Going on to college. Tony, you're going to be successful," Keith's dad said.

I blushed and let his words fill me up. "Thank you."

I was a part of the family; Keith and I were like brothers. I gave his parents a hug and said goodbye.

At night, Keith had some people over in the basement as we listened to some of his thousands of CDs and drank some beers with Coop, Jamie, and some girls. It was quiet as we all seemed to feel the end of the year coming.

Run

I went back to doing what I had to do for college. I took the SATs again, which got me only a slightly better score. I was disappointed when I looked at the score: only fifty points higher, but I had to move on and not dwell on it. My time to enjoy my friends was slipping away.

I continued to hang out with friends. I knew I had to be careful; I couldn't screw up my future. I couldn't disappoint my mom, my family, or myself. So, I didn't drink as much as my friends when we hung out together. I probably should've known something bad was going to happen if I considered past times dealing with cops; that time with Coop and Zima, the times I was fortunate the cops didn't come because I was too high, and when I ran from cops at a party by jumping off a balcony and escaping through woods.

Then there was that time with the police in front of my house …

One day I met up with Jamie, Keith, and some others to hang out and drink. As we walked down a path to meet the other guys, there was a sign that said, "no trespassing." Though we were away from any main roads or homes, there were a few houses we could see, and I was sure they could see us. We all huddled together and laughed about the weekend as they cracked beers and offered me one. "No, I'm alright." *As long as I don't drink, I should be okay and not get into trouble.* I relaxed on the side wearing my baggy jeans and Timberland boots loose and untied, a fashion style which was soon to be detrimental and impact my life.

About an hour later, a neighbor from one of the nearby backyards yelled at us. "Hey, you kids. Get out from over there. There's no trespassing."

"Shut up old man," one of my friends yelled back, laughing at him, and sipping on their beers. I just happened to be looking around: our breaths pluming from our mouths in brisk air, the bare trees around us, the gravel we were standing on, the fences and homes. In the distance were black and blue blurred bodies coming towards us; then they formed into men with hats and gold badges as they came into view. The cops.

"Oh shit …" I said. I guessed the old man called the cops.

"Stop! You're under arrest," the cops yelled.

We scattered. Keith ran towards a backyard to hide behind a bush, waiting to get to his car parked nearby. Jamie jetted in another direction, and a cop ran after him. Others disappeared as I focused on myself.

I can't get caught.

I propelled, kicking up gravel. My usual speed was labored as I pulled up my pants and plodded through mud with my loosely tied boots. Train tracks in the distance were too dangerous to follow. A sky-high fence was coming up, an obstacle like many others in my life. *I can make that.* I jumped on the fence, feeling the cold of the wire on my toes. I turned around to see my shoes were still stuck in the mud. *Damn!* I quickly climbed over without them, landing on sharp gravel under my tender heels. Each step ached. I tried to run, but I was halted by a cop car. I couldn't go any further. I walked to him, defeated. *Fuck!*

"Can I get my shoes?" I asked.

"Yes, you can go get them," he said. I climbed over the fence and got my shoes. Maybe I should've ran. Instead, I jumped back over and walked towards the cop car.

"Have you been drinking? Let me smell your breath," he asked.

"No, I haven't." I said standing outside of the car and breathing into his face.

"You're right. Please put your hands behind your back. I gotta cuff you and put you in the car," he said, putting me in the back.

We pulled off and drove around the neighborhood looking for some of my other friends. They found some of them running around and picked up one and put him in the car with me. We both looked at each other. My heart was pounding out of my chest with fear. *But I'll be okay because I wasn't drinking.*

We were all handcuffed in the police station like criminals. I shook my head in disbelief at the cold metal on my wrists.

After my friends' parents picked them up, Uncle Sam came to get me. Not much was said at home. I spoke to my mother on the phone and explained what happened; I told her I wasn't drinking. She was mad, her voice high pitched, and she gave a sigh of disappointment. I never wanted to disappoint her, so I hung my head low as I sat on the edge of the bed. She continued to reassure me that everything would be okay.

Within a few days it was all in the local newspapers. I didn't think it was serious enough to be in the paper, but there it was in black print for everyone to see and gasp about the town's teenagers and the underage drinking problem. After my Advanced Math class, one of my favorite teachers called me up to her desk at the front of the room.

"I am so disappointed in you. Tony ... you had such promise. You were going to be like Connor," she said, shaking her head. I knew what she meant; I was the smart Black kid like Connor. Over recent years, there weren't many of us in advanced classes on the path to college. I was the only Black kid in her class; in fact, in most of my classes. I immediately remembered Connor recently went to a highly ranked university like I was expected to do. My eyes quivered. *But I didn't drink.*

In the same instance, I saw Amy walking to class down the hall. Our eyes met and I looked away with utter shame. I went on to class and tried to avoid talking about it. *Now she has a boyfriend who's been arrested.*

At home, my friend Jamie called me. "Hey Tony, my dad said our lawyer can work for you too. We feel bad you have to go through this when you did nothing wrong."

I let out a sigh. "Thank you." I was relieved, especially since I couldn't afford a lawyer. I knew I had a better chance with the case now.

When we got to court, my lawyer and I were happy when the police officer said I didn't drink. *Great, I should be okay now.* I sat back and relaxed as I listened to the guilty charges for all my friends.

Then she got to me. "I hereby find the defendant guilty by association for underage drinking, trespassing, and resisting arrest." They gave me the same punishment as my friends. My heart sank.

"Guilty by association? But I wasn't drinking. What is 'guilty by association'? Why am I guilty? Why did I get the same punishment? This can't be. I was careful," I said to the lawyer. I saw my friends in my periphery; their faces also seemed saddened by my verdict.

"Sorry, Anthony. Because you were there, it doesn't matter that you didn't do those things. You are found guilty because of the others around you. I'm sorry," the lawyer said.

I watched as he stood in his black suit, put the folders in his briefcase, and packed up his things to leave with such lack of care and without looking at me as if this had no impact on him. *No. This is going to ruin me. What about college?* I held the disappointment like a sopping wet napkin in my hand. I never wanted to be the young Black boy getting arrested, fitting a stereotypical description. I was supposed to be different.

My friend and his dad came over and they offered to give me a ride home. I was distraught inside, aching, unsure what this would do to me. When I left the court room, I looked at my friends who had their parents. I had to deal with it alone. I got home and called my mom, who breathed deeply and worried, too, but she assured me, "Everything will be okay."

A few weeks after, the guys that got arrested with me met up at a municipal building where we were picked up for our community service working with the garbage men of the town. We spent the next hours, days, and weeks picking up garbage at the back of schools and other buildings, riding around with these garbage men. And as we rode around on sunny days, I was furious at the situation. *Why am I here with them? I was careful. Now what?* I grew worried about my future.[13]

13

I went through the hallways to my English class with some of my other friends. I sat in the classroom, looking at the teacher who was enthused to teach us more and more every day about creative writing. Ideas for stories and poems I wanted to write swirled in my head. I'd look at Ann remembering the poem I wrote for her that she laughed at on the phone when I recited the words "Friends are better than Mercedes Benzs."

The teacher's voice came out of his lips flanked by his thick gray mustache, and his eyes always seemed to be looking at me through his glasses at my seat in the back of the room. I hung on to the teacher's every word, learning how to craft stories, places, and people on paper. I was tapping my feet with my heart racing, waiting to know what he thought of my recent assignment. The night before, at home, I sat at the table, pondering a new story, then became giddy with what I saw and wrote it down to turn in. I looked forward to handing my teacher my story, knowing it was one of the best I'd ever written, possibly the best in class.

At the end of class, I walked up to get the story and learn my grade, expecting him to praise me. He handed me the story with a mediocre grade. I was devastated.

I looked at the grade and the markings of errors on my hard work. Then I looked him in the eyes, and I knew he knew I was disappointed by the way he turned away. But he pointed out my errors and patted me on the shoulder to keep trying. I left that class with my shoulders hunched over and my fists clenched. I gradually felt better when thinking of the next assignment.

As I stepped out of the classroom, I said goodbye to my teacher and friends. I turned and looked over my shoulder with one last look at the desks and brightly lit room … then it all went dark.

My eyes squinted and blinked from the bright light of the hallways. The floor was beneath me as I realized I was on the ground. As I focused, the school nurse called my name, "Tony, are you okay?"

My heart pounded in my chest. It ached as tears rolled down my eyes. *Is this a heart attack? I'm going to die.* The thoughts caused more fear, causing my heart to race faster, and causing more fear. I blinked again. Amy and the teacher were kneeling in front of me with the nurse. *Breathe. Breathe.* I took deep breaths, trying to remember what the doctor told me at the hospital. I looked away from Amy, feeling ashamed for my state in front of her. I was also relieved she was there and that I wasn't alone. I breathed harder and wiped my tears as they helped me up. I tried to move on.

...

Months went by, and everyone was in the hallways; kids were talking about going to college or the last parties of the year. Those hallways were another world outside of the classroom. Everyone hung out with their friends and did what they wanted to do, perhaps what they dreamed of. Those same kids who ran around the halls when I was younger were now the older kids. Lisa's blonde hair swayed as she smiled and skipped to her art class to pursue her talent in painting. I smiled back at her with adoration. I knew that's what she loved, and we just didn't work out.

Other kids went on their way to math club or debate, a couple were guys I used to sing school choir with, and some kids were going to theater practice in the auditorium, while other kids carried instruments to the school band. My friends and mostly everyone else was talking about college. I admired the kids as they went on to do arts or theater or just do what they liked to do. Deep down, I wanted that for myself.

I think we were all trying to be ourselves, whatever we thought that was: the kids in black Goth clothes, the girls with jackets tied around their waist wearing beaded necklaces, and kids with baggy pants. The kids I grew up with roamed the halls too; I never forgot who I was with them, yet I felt I left that piece of me with them.

Here I was, in between it all.

I waved and said hey to most of the kids. Some of them were happy to see me, saying, "Hey, Tony," giving me high fives. Someone came up to me and said I was voted as having the best smile for our graduating year and that I almost won the friendliest. It felt good and warmed me even moments after.

I stood next to Keith and Coop at my locker.

"Yo, what up, bitch?" Keith said, smacking me on the back of my head. We play fought a little. "Dude, you coming over this weekend?"

"Yep. I'll be there," I said pushing him and Coop around as they went off to class. Amy came over.

"Hey," she said smiling.

We held hands by the lockers. "So, what do you want to do this weekend?" I inquired.

"I don't know. What do you want to do?" She coyly smiled.

I watched her brunette hair fall to her shoulders and her plump lips widen into a smile and crease her creamy skin as she talked.

Her friend, Samara, with short brown hair came over. "You guys can come over to my place. My parents are gone."

"Alright. Sounds cool. We can probably go by Keith's too," I said to Amy.

"Okay," she smiled and went to class with her friends. I was getting my books from my locker as the hallways began to clear of the rest of the students.

As I stood at my locker, the back of my neck was hot with scowls from others who didn't seem to like who I was.

I turned to see a group of Black girls covering their mouths, whispering to each other while looking at me, rolling their eyes and curling their mouths up in disgust. One of them was large with short black hair. I turned back to my locker in anger.

Words came from over my shoulder, "You, Oreo. You think you're White?" When I looked, it was the large Black girl with broad shoulders. My fists clinched with anger towards her and everyone else who said that to me. My eyes burned through her. There was no way she could know who I was enough to judge me; I didn't know her.

I looked at my lacrosse jacket and thought back to the day I decided to play, the times I was the only person of color on the team or the other team.

My mom had taken me to a store in Short Hills Mall to buy the clothes I had on; they were usually on sale. I also bought some of these clothes by mowing lawns and shoveling snow. I didn't have the oversized leather jacket and baggy jeans that made the other Black kids look cool like those in hip hop music videos.

I thought of my friends and girlfriend who just left me and how I looked forward to being with them after school.

The words from this Black girl were like I wasn't who I was supposed to be.

They didn't seem to know what or who I was trying to be. I was losing the respect of others with the same color as my skin, in my attempt to not be only defined by the color of my skin. But all the while, I truly loved being a black boy.

I snapped out of it.

"You don't even fucking know me!" I yelled, and I walked off leaving the girl's eyes wide and her mouth opened with astonishment.

After that, only days later, I saw her in the hallways, and she was nice to me by smiling and saying hi. I was aghast. I guess she thought about it and respected me. And I was proud of myself for not changing. I had other things to worry about, like my future.

Goodbye

It was prom time. I pulled up to Amy's house driving my brother Cory's car. It was an all-black Mitsubishi Diamante. I didn't want to rent a limo like we did in previous proms I attended; I wanted to be different. And, to me, it was one the of the nicest cars I could drive. I was pumped with arrogance for having such a car for our senior prom and wearing my rented black tuxedo with the cummerbund and bowtie. I grabbed the corsage and went out the door.

Amy's mom let me wait in the living room. I was giddy; this was our final dance, and I had a girlfriend to take. Amy entered wearing this black velvet dress that was soft to the touch when I hugged her. She looked like this actress Sandra Bullock with her wavy dark hair and smile. I wrapped my arm around her waist as her mom proudly took pictures.

When we got to the dance, music was already blasting, people were sitting at the round tables around the dance floor, some people were on the floor, and people were taking pictures in their fanciest clothes: Girls were wearing their black velvet dresses and guys were in tuxedos and suits. I went over and said what's up to Keith and Coop and their dates as we laughed for a while. Then I headed to a table across the room where Amy and her friends were sitting. As I sat down and saw Keith far away, I already felt it was our last times together as friends as we already started separating. Amy giggled with her friends by my side, seemingly without much thought these may be our last, big moments together.

We all met on the dancefloor, bouncing around to songs of the 90s,[14] and putting our hands on our date's waist for slow dancing. We danced to songs like "This Is How We Do It" by Montell Jordan and "Mo Money Mo

---

14

Problems" by Notorious BIG. Girls sang Spice Girls "Wannabe." Keith and I rapped with each other to "Scenario" like we did when we were younger. Kids were hugging each other and laughing—some drunk, some sober, some too drunk and falling over. Some didn't attend, so you wondered if you'd ever see them again. As the last dance ended, the lights came on and you realized you may never dance with your friends again.

...

I went over to Amy's; my walk up to her house was uneasy.

She opened the door with a bright smile as she normally did. We went down to the basement as I thought through what I wanted to say.

We sat on her couch in the dark room and put on the TV, talking about preparing for college. As the night went on, my heart sped up while we kissed passionately, my hands on her soft skin.

We stopped. I reached into my back pocket and pulled out my wallet with the ring impression, then slid out the old condom. *This is it. This is my last chance to lose my virginity before college.*

"Are we going to have sex?" I asked, holding it in my sweaty hand like I was giving her a piece of me.

She looked at it and burst out laughing. "What? No. I haven't even like touched you."

She was right; I messed up. How could I expect her to do this? I was crushed, flooded with embarrassment, and unable to say a word. There was a silent pause.

"We're going to talk in college, right?" She smiled.

In my mind, I recalled movies like *Animal House* and other conversations I had about college: images of parties filled with beer and all these other girls I may get in college—like it's one big orgy, or you sneak girls into your dorm room, or find a girlfriend you'll have for years after. So many other girls. My school only had a few hundred students; the colleges I checked out had thousands, meaning more girls. My teenage hormones were on fire, eating at my skin while I sat on that couch and considered our future of long-distance phone calls from the dorm room and occasionally seeing each other after several months. All the while, at college, I would be seeing new girls strut around campus in halter tops and short skirts, smiling my way.

I'm not sure if I ever realized what Amy meant to me. At this moment, it felt right, even though we'd had some remarkable times. Times in the hallways at school, in her car, my uncle's truck, Keith's house, and her basement. She was there when I had the panic attack in the hallway at school and at my lacrosse games cheering me on. She stayed even after I got arrested. But I was blinded by a vision of all these girls I could meet in college.

I came back to the moment. I looked in her eyes and started pulling away.

"No, we're not going to talk in college." I said.

It didn't end there, but I was already letting her go.

...

When I got home, I sat at the dining room table reading over the rejection letters from universities. One was from American University; that was my first choice. I had a moment of disappointment that made me sick and caused me to sit down to read the letter again. I put it away. There wasn't much time to worry about those rejections.

I swelled with pride as I looked at the acceptance letters from Lehigh University and Villanova. I let out a sigh of relief; my arrest didn't affect my acceptance. *I made it.* I needed to decide which university to attend.

I recalled the visit to Villanova and how it would be cool to go to their basketball games. But I also remembered being in awe of Lehigh's buildings and campus in the hills, and its high ranking at thirty-three out of the hundreds of universities in the country. A friend told me it was one of the top party schools in the country. *I wouldn't go there to party; I'd focus on my education.*

Tyrone called and said he spoke to my father. When my father found out I was considering Lehigh, he said his sister, my aunt, worked there and could help. I felt uneasy about it as Tyrone told me over the phone. It was bringing my father back into my life. It was like that episode of *The Fresh Prince of Belair*[15] when Will's father came back into his life then left. Sometimes I felt like Carlton from that show, but now I felt closer to Will than ever.

But then I thought my aunt could help me with getting into college and my financial aid. And I knew I needed help; the paperwork itself confused me. Lehigh was also only forty-five minutes from Summit, not far from my family if I ever needed them. I made my choice. I was going to Lehigh, the best college anyone in my family had ever gone to.

At graduation, I sat in my maroon cap and gown as the sun shined down on me and others through clear

---

15

skies. It was a perfect day. I breathed in and watched as my friends and other students had their names called and walked across the stage. Families sat in the bleachers; I noticed my mom and others. The announcer called my name. I walked on clouds, gliding up to the podium as they mentioned I will be going to Lehigh, and I received a scholarship for philanthropy work I did. The rolled-up diploma was light in my hand but heavy with meaning, causing my palms to sweat. I didn't want to lose it or this moment.

Looking out at the crowd of students, I recalled the memories. I knew others were doing the same by the way they looked at the skies. We remembered the times we laughed, cried, and helped each other. We shared memories of pep rallies, football games, and the sports we played. We recalled playing in the snow, going sledding down hills, some of us going skiing, or shoveling. There were thoughts of the plays we acted in, the songs we sang, the music we played, the clubs we joined, and the yearbook we put together. Then we relished those summers at the pool, out of school, and looking forward to going back to school or dreading it. We grew to like people and love them without really understanding the power of it all. Some of us wondered what we'd do next and how, and for a moment, we were nervous and excited. Then we looked around and realized we were all in this together. This was the beginning of another life and the end of our years of youth.

Afterwards, I was beaming as I put my arm around Coop to take pictures with him, Chris, Keith, and Jamie. We all made it here, together. I was grateful to be among them, my friends. I just had one more goodbye to do.

...

As the summer was ending, we went to graduation parties at people's houses across town. I was preparing for college by sitting at my aunt's dining room table contemplating my life: this time I was excited and overjoyed to be going over the course catalog for what classes I'd sign up for, where my dorm would be, and when I should be there. I also started packing for a trip to Florida, in about a month, to spend some time at Mom's place before going to college.

Keith came to pick me up just about every day, and we'd hang out in his pool, drink, play video games, go to the private pool with Coop, and order pizza. We'd fill our days with as much time together as possible as people started to go their separate ways.

I went over to Keith's for one of the last parties. It was filled with all the usual people we'd partied and been friends with over our teenage years.

As the night was ending, I realized it was one of the last parties we'd have at Keith's house. I took an inventory of the times there: we used to sit on those couches to drink and listen to Keith's music, then wake up the next morning on those same couches to Keith's dad doing sit ups and telling us to clean up our mess of pizza boxes and empty beer cans. There was the other side room with the couch where Keith had sex with some girl, and I hooked up with another girl in the closet. The pool outside was the only pool any of our friends had, and we were in it every chance we had.

Then there were the people I'd grown up with.

I said goodbye to some of my other friends as they were preparing to go away to college soon. Hakim had his senior year of high school coming up, but I knew he'd always be a part of my life because he was family. Coop was going to Muhlenberg college only a few minutes away from Lehigh, so I knew I'd see him again. Keith was going to college somewhere in New York. I didn't know how I'd ever see him again.

After the night was over and everyone went home, Keith drove me to Grandma's house for my flight to Florida the next day. We sat in his black jeep laughing about nothing and blasting some of our favorite music. We pulled up to my grandparents' back parking lot. We got out and walked up to the porch with my bags. There was a pause and all we could hear were the night's sounds: gentle breeze, crickets, and lights buzzing. I gave him a handshake and wrapped my arm around him. He got into his car, gave me one more look, then drove away into the moon light. I went to sit in my grandmother's living room in the darkness, thinking of saying goodbye to Keith and my other friends, feeling like an era of living in Summit was ending. The times I'd spent in this living room as a child with family dancing around or eating dinner was long over, and I was growing up even more in that moment just realizing it.[16]

16

Failure

I was at my mom's apartment in Pembroke Pines, Florida, soaking up the sun on the balcony. It was two weeks before I would fly back up north to go to school at Lehigh. We were doing a lot of planning for the trip and college life. That day, Mom, Norman, and Aunt Esther were out doing some grocery shopping while I was in my room putting some stuff in a trunk we just bought a few days ago: a blanket, clothes, and school supplies. Tyrone told me that I needed a trunk, something he learned he needed from his first couple of years at college.

The phone rang. I quickly picked it up and headed out to the balcony near the parking lot. It was Aunt Joan, my dad's sister. This was something new talking to her. I didn't have many conversations with relatives on my father's side since I never really spoke to my father. But a few months ago, he found out I was going to Lehigh and put me in touch with Aunt Joan who worked at the school and was helping me with financial aid, paperwork, and other things. I was awaiting her call to confirm everything was okay.

"Hi, Tony," she said with a gentle tone.

"Hi, Aunt Joan. How are things?" I said excited to hear from her, thankful that she'd been helping me.

"I'm fine." She let out a sigh. "I have something to tell you."

My heart was beating fast. My parents' car was pulling up to the apartment as I was on the phone on the balcony.

"What's wrong? What happened?" I probed nervously. My heart raced and my hand trembled.

"Sorry Tony, your financial aid didn't come through. There was something wrong with the paperwork and it took too long. I'm sorry, I don't think you'll be able to go to college."

I couldn't breathe as tears filled up my eyes. *No, I'm not going to be anything.* I messed up that paperwork; I didn't know that would be the end for me. I tried so hard for so long. I got good grades, stayed in Summit for my final year, got arrested, applied, and got accepted into great schools for it to all come falling on me. What was I going to do without college?

TO BE CONTINUED…

Find out what I do next, what happens to Tyrone, more about my father, and whether I see any of my friends again. How does life go on? All in book two: Getting Higher …

Letter to the Reader

Dear reader,

Thank you for reading my dream come true. I encourage you all to follow any dreams you have.

I loved my time growing up in Summit and speak proudly of it. I fondly consider those people that continue to be a part of my story.

To those I didn't mention in the story, I didn't forget you and your impact on my life. Unfortunately, I had to cut some parts and people to focus on others. I thank you.

To those who enjoyed and are currently enjoying your time at school and teenage years, savor every second. Hold the memories as long as you desire.

To those who were made fun of, treated poorly, felt ugly, like they didn't fit in, felt misunderstood, or felt less than others, I'm truly sorry you felt that way. I apologize if I was the reason for it. You are beautiful and better; you always were and will be. I see you now, succeeding and smiling.

I wrote this story to entertain but also show how a life story starts. High school is the beginning; there is more to come. I will show you.

Sincerely,

Anthony Ellis

Media & Information

Instagram: instragram.com/anthonyellisauthor

Facebook: facebook.com/anthonyellisauthor

YouTube: Climbing The Summit Book

https://www.youtube.com/playlist?list=PLdXZy7E5w-_cOrrFuX6A1TH3e6xYxXeHl

References/Footnotes

*= QR Codes

1. *The Cosby Show* – Season two, episode three: "Happy Anniversary:
https://www.youtube.com/watch?v=XSvGdfOfLFw&list=PLdXZy7E5w-_cOrrFuX6A1TH3e6xYxXeHl&index=1&ab_channel=cosbyshow

2. *80s Music playlist:
https://www.youtube.com/watch?v=oRdxUFDoQe0&list=PLdXZy7E5w-_cOrrFuX6A1TH3e6xYxXeHl&index=3&ab_channel=michaeljacksonVEVO

3.

4. *Michael Jackson - "Beat It"*:
https://www.youtube.com/watch?v=oRdxUFDoQe0&list=PLdXZy7E5w-_cOrrFuX6A1TH3e6xYxXeHl&index=3&ab_channel=michaeljacksonVEVO

5. Whitney Houston - "I Wanna Dance With Somebody":
https://www.youtube.com/watch?v=eH3giaIzONA&list=PLdXZy7E

5w-
_cOrrFuX6A1TH3e6xYxXeHl&index=3&ab_channel=whitneyhous
tonVEVO
6.   A-ha - "Take On Me":
https://www.youtube.com/watch?v=djV11Xbc914&list=PLdXZy7E
5w-_cOrrFuX6A1TH3e6xYxXeHl&index=4&ab_channel=a-ha
7.   Wham - "Wake Me Up Before You Go-Go":
https://www.youtube.com/watch?v=pIgZ7gMze7A&list=PLdXZy7
E5w-
_cOrrFuX6A1TH3e6xYxXeHl&index=5&ab_channel=WhamVEV
O
8.   Chaka Khan - "I Feel For You":
https://www.youtube.com/watch?v=YW0sxgYAmLM&list=PLdXZ
y7E5w-
_cOrrFuX6A1TH3e6xYxXeHl&index=6&ab_channel=RHINO
9.   Anita Baker - "Giving You The Best That I Got":
https://www.youtube.com/watch?v=rUSddpvB4X0&list=PLdXZy7
E5w-
_cOrrFuX6A1TH3e6xYxXeHl&index=7&ab_channel=koollatter
10.   Michael Jackson - "Billie Jean":
https://www.youtube.com/watch?v=Zi_XLOBDo_Y&list=PLdXZy
7E5w-_cOrrFuX6A1TH3e6xYxXeHl&index=10
11.   *Maurice Williams and The Zodiacs - "Stay":
https://www.youtube.com/watch?v=o1Z_hskvz1M&list=PLdXZy7E
5w-
_cOrrFuX6A1TH3e6xYxXeHl&index=9&ab_channel=BearWalken
12.   *Dirty Dancing - Maurice Williams and The Zodiacs -
"Stay":
https://www.youtube.com/watch?v=p6b2d7jge5I&list=PLdXZy7E5
w-
_cOrrFuX6A1TH3e6xYxXeHl&index=10&ab_channel=0000MATI
NA
13.   Dave Matthews Band - Ants Marching:
https://www.youtube.com/watch?v=MNgJBIx-
hK8&list=PLdXZy7E5w-
_cOrrFuX6A1TH3e6xYxXeHl&index=11&ab_channel=davematthe
wsbandVEVO

14. *Early 90s playlist:
https://www.youtube.com/watch?v=010KyIQjkTk&list=PLdXZy7E
5w-_cOrrFuX6A1TH3e6xYxXeHl&index=13
15. Kris Kross - "Jump":
https://www.youtube.com/watch?v=010KyIQjkTk&list=PLdXZy7E
5w-_cOrrFuX6A1TH3e6xYxXeHl&index=13
16. Wreckx N Effect - "Rump Shaker":
https://www.youtube.com/watch?v=zdLvauICvPM&list=PLdXZy7
E5w-
_cOrrFuX6A1TH3e6xYxXeHl&index=13&ab_channel=TheGetDo
wnRecords
17. Aly Us - "Follow Me":
https://www.youtube.com/watch?v=5oiO5A8OOlk&list=PLdXZy7
E5w-
_cOrrFuX6A1TH3e6xYxXeHl&index=14&ab_channel=ajcgn4
18. Tribe Called Quest - "Scenario":
https://www.youtube.com/watch?v=Q6TLWqn82J4&list=PLdXZy7
E5w-
_cOrrFuX6A1TH3e6xYxXeHl&index=15&ab_channel=TribeCalle
dQuestVEVO
19. Boyz II Men - "End Of The Road":
https://www.youtube.com/watch?v=zDKO6XYXioc&list=PLdXZy
7E5w-
_cOrrFuX6A1TH3e6xYxXeHl&index=16&ab_channel=BoyzIIMen
VEVO
20. A Tribe Called Quest - "Check The Rhime":
https://www.youtube.com/watch?v=1QWEPdgS3As&list=PLdXZy
7E5w-
_cOrrFuX6A1TH3e6xYxXeHl&index=21&ab_channel=TribeCalle
dQuestVEVO
21. *Rap songs -
https://www.youtube.com/watch?v=PBwAxmrE194&list=PLdXZy7
E5w-_cOrrFuX6A1TH3e6xYxXeHl&index=23
22. Wu-Tang - "C.R.E.A.M.":
https://www.youtube.com/watch?v=PBwAxmrE194&list=PLdXZy7
E5w-_cOrrFuX6A1TH3e6xYxXeHl&index=23

23. Wu-Tang - "Protect Ya Neck":
https://www.youtube.com/watch?v=R0IUR4gkPIE&list=PLdXZy7E5w-_cOrrFuX6A1TH3e6xYxXeHl&index=23&ab_channel=WuTangClanVEVO

24. Warren G & Nate Dogg - "Regulator":
https://www.youtube.com/watch?v=1plPyJdXKIY&list=PLdXZy7E5w-_cOrrFuX6A1TH3e6xYxXeHl&index=23&ab_channel=WarrenGVEVO

25. Notorious B.I.G. - "Juicy":
https://www.youtube.com/watch?v=_JZom_gVfuw&list=PLdXZy7E5w-_cOrrFuX6A1TH3e6xYxXeHl&index=24&ab_channel=TheNotoriousB.I.G.

26. *Jungle Fever - Gator's Last Dance:
https://www.youtube.com/watch?v=xhn7kToBRAM&list=PLdXZy7E5w-_cOrrFuX6A1TH3e6xYxXeHl&index=25&ab_channel=memories2musicLLCProductions

27. Eric Clapton - "Tears In Heaven":
https://www.youtube.com/watch?v=JxPj3GAYYZ0&list=PLdXZy7E5w-_cOrrFuX6A1TH3e6xYxXeHl&index=27&ab_channel=Epitaph

28. *Dave Matthews Band - "Crash":
https://www.youtube.com/watch?v=k7in-9E3ImQ&list=PLdXZy7E5w-_cOrrFuX6A1TH3e6xYxXeHl&index=28&ab_channel=davematthewsbandVEVO

29. *Tracy Chapman - "Fast Car":
https://www.youtube.com/watch?v=AIOAlaACuv4&list=PLdXZy7E5w-_cOrrFuX6A1TH3e6xYxXeHl&index=29&ab_channel=TracyChapman

30. Songs of the 90s playlist:
https://www.youtube.com/watch?v=0hiUuL5uTKc&list=PLdXZy7E5w-_cOrrFuX6A1TH3e6xYxXeHl&index=26

31.   Montell Jordan - "This Is How We Do It":
https://www.youtube.com/watch?v=0hiUuL5uTKc&list=PLdXZy7E5w-_cOrrFuX6A1TH3e6xYxXeHl&index=26

32.   Notorious B.I.G. - "Mo Money Mo Problems":
https://www.youtube.com/watch?v=gUhRKVIjJtw&list=PLdXZy7E5w-_cOrrFuX6A1TH3e6xYxXeHl&index=31&ab_channel=TheNotoriousB.I.G.

33.   Spice Girls - "Wannabe":
https://www.youtube.com/watch?v=gJLIiF15wjQ&list=PLdXZy7E5w-_cOrrFuX6A1TH3e6xYxXeHl&index=32&ab_channel=SpiceGirlsVEVO

34.   Donna Summer - "Last Dance":
https://www.youtube.com/watch?v=G5rJunb4sIk&list=PLdXZy7E5w-_cOrrFuX6A1TH3e6xYxXeHl&index=37&ab_channel=JadeDiscoHD

35.   Fresh Prince Of Belair - Will's Father Leaves:
https://www.youtube.com/watch?v=PI4Mv8R0mE0&list=PLdXZy7E5w-_cOrrFuX6A1TH3e6xYxXeHl&index=38&ab_channel=CharlesBentley

36.   The Breakfast Club - Ending Scene:
https://www.youtube.com/watch?v=Sv1I4q6lOpo&list=PLdXZy7E5w-_cOrrFuX6A1TH3e6xYxXeHl&index=39&ab_channel=ChristopheGADEA

Made in United States
North Haven, CT
01 November 2022

26187021R10102